The Woodworker's Technique Bible

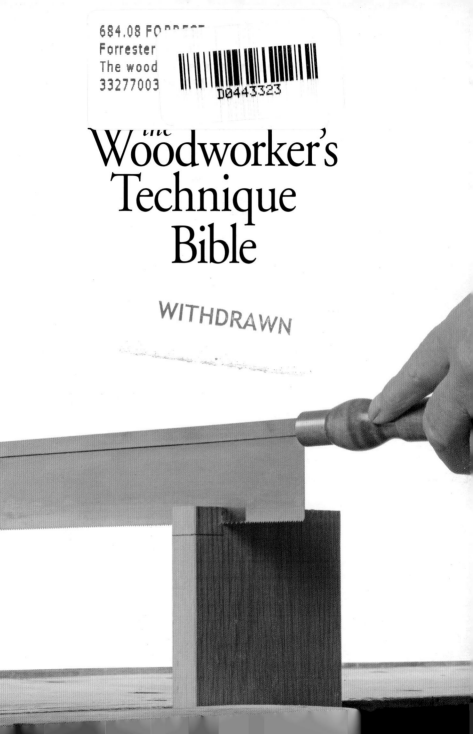

the Woodworker's Technique Bible

The *essential illustrated reference*

Paul Forrester

FIREFLY BOOKS

A FIREFLY BOOK

Published by Firefly Books Ltd. 2009

Copyright © 2009 Quarto Inc.

First printing

Publisher Cataloging-in-Publication Data (U.S.)
Forrester, Paul.
   The woodworker's technique bible : the essential illustrated reference / Paul Forrester.
[256] p. : col. photos. ; cm.
Includes index.
Summary: A step-by-step guide to woodwork techniques, including cutting and shaping wood, joining and finishing, veneering, woodcarving and woodturning.
ISBN-13: 978-1-55407-488-4
ISBN-10: 1-55407-488-6
1. Woodwork -- Handbooks, manuals, etc. I. Title.
684.08 dc22   TT180.F677 2009

**Library and Archive Canada Cataloguing
in Publication**
Forrester, Paul, 1944–
   The woodworker's technique bible : the essential illustrated reference / Paul Forrester.
Includes index.
ISBN-13: 978-1-55407-488-4
ISBN-10: 1-55407-488-6
1. Woodwork. I. Title.
TT185.F67 2009   684'.08   C2009-901874-8

Published in the United States by
Firefly Books (U.S.) Inc.
P.O. Box 1338, Ellicott Station
Buffalo, New York 14205

Published in Canada by
Firefly Books Ltd.
66 Leek Crescent
Richmond Hill, Ontario L4B 1H1

Conceived, designed and produced by
Quarto Publishing plc
The Old Brewery
6 Blundell Street
London N7 9BH

For Quarto Inc.:
Editor & designer: Michelle Pickering
Proofreader: Claire Waite Brown
Indexer: Dorothy Frame
Art director: Caroline Guest
Photographers: Paul Forrester, Laura Forrester
Picture researcher: Sarah Bell

Creative director: Moira Clinch
Publisher: Paul Carslake
QUA: WWB

Color separation by Pica Digital Pte Ltd, Singapore
Printed by Midas Printing International Ltd, China

Contents

1
Wood and the workshop

Choosing wood and setting up
a safe workshop

Characteristics of wood

Each species of wood has its own distinctive characteristics, though many share similar colors, grain patterns or textures. Hardwoods are favored for their strength, decorative effects, wide range of colors and durability. Softwoods tend to be cheaper, and are often seen as functional materials for building and construction. The terms softwood and hardwood often cause confusion because they refer to the botanical characteristics of the tree, not whether the wood is soft or hard. Some hardwoods are very soft, such as balsa wood, while some softwoods can be quite hard, such as yew.

Tree growth

A tree grows by adding to its circumference each year, as well as to its height and breadth. At the center of the trunk is the pith or medulla—the remains of the sapling from which the tree grew. Then follows a series of growth rings, usually formed annually. These rings result from the change in growth speed through the seasons of the year, from pale, lighter earlywood to dark, denser latewood. The rings are more visible in temperate zones, where the seasons differ more markedly. Horizontal medullary rays radiate from the center of the tree. On the outside, the cambium layer forms new wood, and the bast and bark ensure annual growth.

Heartwood and sapwood

The wood near the center of the trunk, the heartwood, forms the structural support of the tree. The outer area transmits food and is called sapwood. In some species, only the heartwood is used for woodwork, because the sapwood is weak and prone to fungal and insect attack; in other species, there is little difference, other than color, between the two. The proportion of sapwood to heartwood varies from species to species.

Sapwood

Heartwood

Growth ring

Cambium

Bast

Bark

Pith

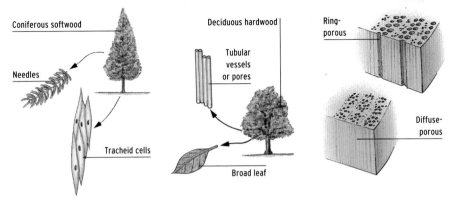

Coniferous softwood

Needles

Tracheid cells

Deciduous hardwood

Tubular vessels or pores

Broad leaf

Ring-porous

Diffuse-porous

Softwoods and hardwoods

Softwoods come from coniferous trees with needles (instead of leaves) that tend to remain during winter. Softwoods are composed of short tracheid cells; food and moisture are transmitted between adjacent cell walls. Softwoods may also have vessels or pores, like hardwoods, but these are generally channels for resin.

Hardwoods come from deciduous trees; their leaves are shed in temperate climates each winter. The tree structure is made from long tubular vessels or pores that allow the tree to conduct moisture and food vertically; horizontal medullary rays carry food in a radial direction. Hardwoods can be either ring- or diffuse-porous. Ring-porous trees show clear growth rings marking the seasons, while diffuse-porous trees live in areas where growth is year-round.

Grain

Grain is the pattern created by the arrangement of the wood fibers. The finest woods are favored for their straight grain, which is the easiest to work with. Other types of grain include wavy, curling, spiraling and irregular. Interlocking grain, with its direction almost impossible to predict, is the most challenging to work with. The texture of the grain varies from coarse-grained woods that have large, open pores to fine-grained woods that have small, close pores; the latter are easier to bring to a high, blemish-free finish.

The consistency of the grain depends on the contrast between earlywood and latewood. Tropical woods grow more evenly throughout the year, so the contrast is only slight, and such woods are often favored for their even grain. The contrast is more significant in temperate regions, being pleasing to the eye but occasionally frustrating to work.

Coarse, wavy grain with distinctive medullary rays

Medium-to-coarse, interlocking grain

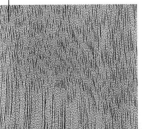

Fine, even, straight grain

Buying wood

Wood is extracted from the forest as logs that are then sawn into boards and seasoned (dried) before being sold. Always check the wood carefully before buying, because faults may be found due to growth defects, bad felling or poor seasoning. Avoid wood with knots, cracks, splits, warping, stains, or signs of fungus or mildew.

▶ Cutting methods

Logs are converted into boards at the sawmill using a variety of cutting arrangements. Different cuts produce boards with surfaces that are either tangential or radial to the growth rings of the log. Boards cut tangentially are called plainsawn; the growth rings meet the surface at an angle of less than 30 degrees (US) or 45 degrees (Europe), producing a characteristic flame-shaped pattern. Boards cut radially are called quartersawn; the growth rings meet the surface at an angle greater than 60 degrees (US) or 45 degrees (Europe). In the US, when growth rings meet the surface at an angle between 30 and 60 degrees, the boards are called riftsawn.

Tangential section

Radial section

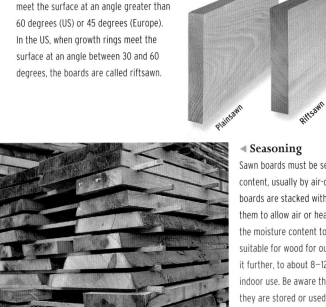

Plainsawn

Riftsawn

Quartersawn

◀ Seasoning

Sawn boards must be seasoned to reduce their moisture content, usually by air-drying and/or kiln-drying. The boards are stacked with spacers (called stickers) between them to allow air or heat to circulate. Air-drying reduces the moisture content to about 16 percent, which is suitable for wood for outside use; kiln-drying reduces it further, to about 8–12 percent, which is suitable for indoor use. Be aware that boards will expand or shrink if they are stored or used in an atmosphere that is too wet or too dry, because their moisture content will adjust to the surroundings.

▶ Shrinkage and distortion

Wood tends to move across the grain rather than along the grain, so boards shrink across their width and thickness as they dry, but hardly at all along their length. If you look at the end of a board, you will see the growth rings (more pronounced on some woods than others). A rule of thumb is that growth rings will try to straighten out as the wood dries. This gives you an indication of which way the board will shrink and distort. A plainsawn board with long growth rings is likely to distort more than a quartersawn or riftsawn board with short growth rings.

Plainsawn boards have long, uneven growth rings running along the surface, so they tend to shrink widthwise and cup away from the tree's original heart.

Quartersawn boards have short growth rings perpendicular to the surface, causing minimal shrinkage and distortion.

Square sections with perpendicular growth rings have optimum dimensional stability.

Square sections with diagonal growth rings tend to go rhomboid.

Rough-sawn or planed

Boards are sold either rough-sawn or planed. Planed boards may be PAR (planed all round) or PBS (planed both sides, with the edges rough-sawn). Although more expensive, it is easier to check planed boards for faults. The best woods are those without defects, such as knots or splits. The best hardwoods are graded as FAS (Firsts and Seconds). The best softwoods are the Appearance grades; Common grades are good for DIY tasks; stress-graded softwood is for structural use.

Dimensions

Softwoods are available in standard dimensions, referred to as either nominal or dressed. The nominal dimension relates to the rough-sawn size of the board; the dressed dimension refers to the planed size. Suppliers often quote the nominal size, regardless of whether the boards are rough-sawn or planed, so always double-check because the dressed size may be up to $1/4$ in. (6mm) less than the nominal size. The length of board is always as stated.

The size of hardwood boards varies widely, depending on the species and the source, although hardwood is also sometimes available in standard dimensions.

All softwoods and most hardwoods are supplied straight-edged, making it simple to estimate how much you need. However, some hardwoods may have one or two waney (irregular) edges. Suppliers measure the widest and narrowest points and then average out the width.

Planed maple

Wastage factor

Always buy more wood than you need for a project, because there will certainly be wastage and you may make mistakes. You will lose up to $1/4$ in. (6mm) off the thickness when planing rough-sawn boards in the workshop. Sapwood and defects may also increase wastage rates. Adding a 30 percent wastage factor is a good idea.

Rough-sawn maple

Wood directory

Of the many thousands of woods that exist, only a very small proportion is available commercially. Nevertheless, there is still a large choice available, and very often there are several species that may be equally suitable for the job at hand—a table, for example, may look just as good in oak as in elm, and serve exactly the same purpose. Furniture makers prefer to use strong, straight-grained woods for legs and rails, more decorative, softer woods for chair seats, and stable boards, ideally quartersawn, that will not bend and buckle for panels. Carvers like ornate wood, but prefer it to be even-grained to reduce the risk of tearing. Turners use almost anything, especially if the grain and color are distinctive. The following woods are a small but representative selection of those in fairly common use. An oil finish has been applied to enhance the natural grain pattern.

▶ Pine

Pines (*Pinus* spp.) and similar softwoods, such as firs (*Abies* spp.) and spruces (*Picea* spp.), grow quickly and are widely employed in building and joinery. They are now also being used increasingly in furniture production. They can be used in solid or veneer form, or as a core wood faced with hardwood veneers. The color of pine ranges from white or yellow to shades of pink. Usually straight-grained and often knotty, pine is generally fine or medium in texture. It is easy to work with either hand or machine tools, and its relative softness makes it easy to carve.

Western white pine (*Pinus monticola*)

White pine (*Pinus strobus*)

Southern yellow pine (*Pinus palustris*)

Scots pine or European redwood (*Pinus sylvestris*)

American beech (*Fagus grandiflora*)

European beech (*Fagus sylvatica*)

American elm (*Ulmus americana*)

▲ Beech

Beech (*Fagus* spp.) is a hard, very versatile, close-grained hardwood with a straight, even grain pattern. The color ranges from a whitish or pale brown to a darker reddish brown. The wood is used mainly for furniture, particularly chair frames, because it lends itself to bending and shaping. It is also suitable for turning. Beech can be stained to imitate other woods, such as mahogany, walnut and oak.

▼ Birch

A close-grained hardwood, birch (*Betula* spp.) is used for furniture, paneling and the production of plywood. It is also excellent for turnery and bending. Birch is straight-grained and fine-textured. Yellow birch has reddish yellow heartwood and pale sapwood; European birch is a uniform creamy white to pale tan. Birch is sometimes finished to imitate other woods.

▲ ▼ Elm

Elm (*Ulmus* spp.) works and bends exceptionally well. American elm has a coarse but even texture, straight grain with a little interlocking, and is pale brown in color. European elm has a coarse, swirling grain and luscious colors. This hardwood works and bends exceptionally well, and is particularly suitable for chair seats, tabletops and cabinets.

Yellow birch (*Betula alleghaniensis*)

European birch (*Betula pendula*)

European elm (*Ulmus hollandica*)

American white oak (*Quercus alba*)

American red oak (*Quercus rubra*)

European white oak (*Quercus robur*)

▲ Oak

Oak (*Quercus* spp.) is a tough, durable hardwood, with excellent woodworking properties. The white oaks are considered superior to the red, because they have a finer texture. White oak is a consistent tan to straw color; red oak has biscuit-pink to reddish brown heartwood. The American oaks have medium-to-coarse, straight grain; European oak is renowned for its coarse, wavy grain, with distinctive medullary rays.

▼ Maple

Maple (*Acer* spp.) has a variety of uses, from furniture to flooring. The color ranges from white to light brown, and there are two varieties available commercially. Sugar maple (or hard maple) is the harder of the two; soft maple (or red maple) is not, in reality, that much softer, but is much easier to work and has a darker color. Both types of this hardwood have a fine, even texture; the grain is straight to wavy.

▼ Lime or basswood

Lime or basswood (*Tilia* spp.) is a pale, creamy yellow hardwood that is extremely easy to work. Evenly textured and close-grained, with virtually no grain pattern, lime is considered to be the best wood for fine detail carving.

Sugar maple (*Acer saccharum*)

Soft maple (*Acer rubrum*)

Lime/basswood (*Tilia americana*)

Teak (*Tectona grandis*)

African mahogany (*Khaya ivorensis*)

American mahogany
(*Swietenia macrophylla*)

▲ Teak

Teak (*Tectona grandis*) is a durable hardwood with good weathering properties. Its color ranges from golden yellow to darker brown. Being naturally oily, it is suitable for decking on boats and other situations exposed to moisture. However, the oily nature of teak can cause problems with finishes. It has straight or wavy grain, with a medium-to-coarse texture that tends to be uneven.

▲ Mahogany

Mahogany (*Swietenia* spp., *Khaya* spp., *Melia* spp.) has a rich color and figure that is second to none. It is a joy to work with and takes a fine finish. Color varies from pale pink to reddish brown and deep brown. The grain can be straight, but also interlocked. Mahogany is a favorite wood for pianos, and the deep red variety used for the backs of guitars and other stringed instruments is known as fiddleback mahogany. Cuban mahogany (*Swietenia mahogani*) is now all but extinct.

Conservation

■ Most concerned woodworkers see it as their responsibility to use wood from a sustainable source. The Forest Stewardship Council (FSC) is the most prominent of several organizations that operate certification programs for wood from well-managed forests. However, the range of available species is still limited, with certification very difficult in some parts of the world.

■ A number of organizations keep track of species considered at risk of extinction. Foremost among these is CITES (Convention on International Trade in Endangered Species), which produces lists, called Appendices, of endangered woods sold commercially. Species listed in CITES Appendix I are defined as being threatened by extinction; those listed in Appendix II are endangered and their trade is controlled. If you plan to use a wood that is not FSC-certified or similar, check its endangered status on the CITES lists. If it is at risk, choose an alternative.

■ Whenever possible, it is good practice to use recycled materials of your own or bought from salvage yards in the form of boards or furniture that can be dismantled. This is the only ethical way to use the rarest woods.

American walnut (*Juglans nigra*)

European walnut (*Juglans regia*)

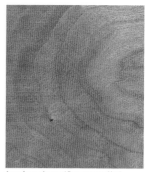
American cherry (*Prunus serotina*)

▲ Walnut

The color of walnut (*Juglans* spp.) ranges from dark, almost black, heartwood to pale, gray sapwood. A wax finish is traditional for this hardwood because of its natural beauty. Walnut is also very strong, so it can be fashioned into attractive shapes—for example, highly figured chair frames, with the grain running through. It has a uniform texture, with straight or curving grain, and is easy to work.

▼ Ash

Ash (*Fraxinus* spp.) is a strong hardwood with a distinctive coarse, straight, open grain. Its color varies from reddish brown and creamy pale brown to dark brown; the wood tends to yellow with age. Ash is renowned for its flexibility, which lends it well to furniture making, interior joinery and boat building. Ash is an excellent wood to turn, and its good shock resistance makes it an ideal wood for tool handles and sports equipment.

▲ ▼ Cherry

Cherry (*Prunus* spp.) is a strong, fine-grained, even-textured hardwood with a very pleasant smell when worked. Its color ranges from an attractive creamy pink to brown, and the color becomes even richer as the wood ages. Cherry bends and glues well, and polishes to a high finish. It is good for furniture making, boat interiors, turning and inlay.

American ash
(*Fraxinus americana*)

European ash (*Fraxinus excelsior*)

European cherry (*Prunus avium*)

▼ Special effects

Although many woodworkers yearn for straight-grained wood that is easy to plane and neat to work, there is often an irresistible challenge in working with trickier boards and wood that displays the most decorative grain, patterning, color and texture. The majority of these effects are utilized in the form of veneers (see page 18), but woodturners and carvers also like to employ burls, figured and diseased sections. Given the opportunity, most furniture makers will opt for the stability and beauty of quartersawn boards.

Figured wood

Figure is the term used to describe the decorative pattern on a wood surface caused by grain, color variations, branch growth, growth stresses or other factors. Unusual features such as a burl—hard, swirling scar tissue formed by a wound to the tree's skin—contribute to interesting figure in wood. Such wood is highly prized for veneers and decorative items.

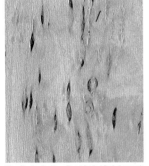

The flecks in Karelian birch (*Betula* spp.) are believed to be caused by insect attack or some other shock or injury.

The tiny, pithy explosions of bird's-eye figuring, notably in maple (*Acer* spp.), may be caused by insect attack.

The fiddleback figuring in this sapele (*Entandrophragma cylindricum*) transforms the surface when viewed from different angles.

Quartersawn red oak (*Quercus rubra*) reveals flamed medullary rays that can vary greatly in pattern and effect.

The tight mottling of lacewood figuring, most commonly found in London plane (*Platanus acerifolia*), is revealed by quartersawing.

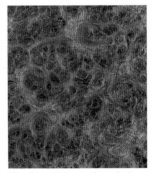

The golden pattern of amboyna burl (*Pterocarpus indicus*) resembles a microscopic view of bacteria hurtling around a slide.

Veneers and inlays

Veneers are thin slices of wood, used for decorative or constructional purposes. Wood is converted into decorative veneer because some species are too rare or expensive to be used as solid wood, or their structure makes them unsuitable to be used in solid form. When glued to a stable substrate, they produce fine colors, shapes, patterns and textures that may be impossible to achieve using solid wood.

Veneers

Decorative veneers are usually quite thin—from $1/64$ to $1/32$ in. (0.5 to 1mm). Constructional veneers are used in the production of plywood or laminated shapes and are generally much thicker, from about $1/16$ to $1/8$ in. (2 to 3mm). The best veneers are graded as face quality; poorer ones are graded as backing quality. Veneers are stacked in sequence from the slicer so that patterns can be matched, so always take them consecutively from the pack, and buy enough to complete a project. Stringings and bandings are plain or patterned strips of veneer that can be used as a decorative divider (stringing) or border (banding).

From left to right: cherry, zebrano, pine, pomelle, tropical olive, olive ash, Brazilian rosewood and aspen veneers.

A range of veneer stringings and bandings.

A selection of marquetry inlays.

Inlays

Inlay motifs are bought readymade to inset in a veneer surface or for use in marquetry. If possible, the inlay should be the same thickness as the veneer for even pressure during gluing. Traditionally, other materials, such as mother-of-pearl and brass, have also been used for veneer inlay.

Manmade boards

Much of the household furniture bought today is manufactured from manmade boards, such as plywood, particle board and fiberboard. These materials are cheap and often veneered with expensive woods that in the solid are not available. They come in large widths that are stable, so there is no problem with movement in a centrally heated environment. All are available in standard dimensions.

MDF is notable for its ability to work well and hold a fine edge.

Plywood

Plywood is formed by gluing sheets of construction veneer together. Usually, the grain of each sheet (ply) is set at right angles to its neighbor, with an odd number of plies used. The more plies, the greater the strength—multi-ply is stronger than three-ply, for example. Birch plywood is regarded as superior in quality. The face ply of the board is graded by appearance, with A grade being the best. Blockboard is a type of plywood, with an inner core of strips of wood rather than veneer. Plywood is made using different grades of glue for interior, exterior or marine use. Flexible plywood, which has three plies with the grain running in the same direction, is also available.

Particle board

Particle board is made from bonded wood chips and is commonly referred to as chipboard. Cheap but also brittle, it is weaker than the other manmade boards. The surfaces may be featureless or decorative.

Fiberboard

MDF (medium-density fiberboard) is formed from bonded wood fibers. It is available in many surface finishes, takes veneer well and is easy to work with. Flexible MDF is grooved on one side to allow it to bend. Hardboard is a strong, high-density fiberboard; one or both faces may be smooth.

⚠ **Warning**

The resin used to bond manmade boards has a devastating effect on tools unless they are tungsten-carbide tipped. The dust produced, especially from MDF, is harmful, so a good dust mask is essential.

From left to right: hardboard, three-ply board, three-layer particle board, decorative plywood, MDF and birch multi-ply.

Planning a workshop

Your workshop should be clean, well organized and safe. Aim for as much space as possible. Even if you only use hand tools at the moment, keep in mind that you may need space later for machines. Arrange workbenches and machines so that you are able to move freely from one to another, and make sure that there is sufficient room to feed a workpiece into a machine at one side and extract it at the other. Appropriate storage solutions for tools and wood are also an important consideration.

◄ Wall-mounted tool storage

The best way to store hand tools is to hang them from pegs on walls or wall-mounted boards. Some woodworkers paint an outline shadow of each tool on the board, so that they can see at a glance if one is missing. Chisels and gouges can be stored in slotted blocks.

► Shelving for tools

Edged tools and power tools can be stored in cupboards, or on open shelving so that they are easy to see and reach. You can fasten a lip at the outer edge of shelves, and tilt the shelves slightly, to prevent tools from falling off.

◄ Heat and humidity

Movement in wood can be a great problem, so you need to control the heat and humidity in the workshop. Ideally, boards should be given a final conditioning at the same temperature and humidity as the rooms where they are likely to end up. If possible, store your wood for some weeks in the house itself, or try to match those conditions in the workshop. Use a moisture meter to check the moisture content of the wood.

Anatomy of a workshop

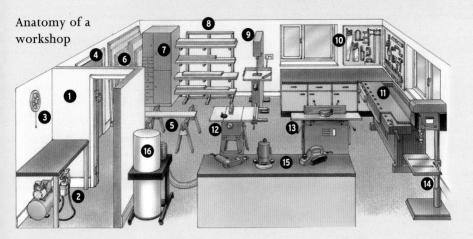

1 Finishing room
You need a separate area that can be kept clean from dust and debris.

2 Spraying equipment
Store this in the finishing area.

3 Extractor fan
Some form of air extraction is essential when applying finishes.

4 Main entrance
Keep it clear. This space will come in handy for rough marking, cutting and assembly.

5 Sawhorses
A couple of sawhorses are useful for rough sawing.

6 Manmade board storage
Store on edge, preferably in a rack at a slight angle; support thin boards with thicker ones.

7 Storage for supplies
Store finishes, hardware, glue and other supplies on shelves and in drawers, ideally in a fireproof cupboard.

8 Wood storage
Use an open shelving system so that air can circulate and you can easily see what stock you have.

9 Bandsaw
Place this against a wall and roll it into the room when necessary.

10 Hand tool storage
Hang tools from pegs on the wall, in slotted blocks, on open shelving or in a cupboard.

11 Workbench
Position it near a window for good lighting, and near the central sawing and planing machines.

12 Table saw
This should be at the center of the workshop, with plenty of space all around it for maneuvering the wood.

13 Jointer planer
Place this near the table saw for easy workflow. It can be positioned against a wall, but make sure that there is adequate infeed and outfeed space.

14 Drill press
Position this against a wall.

15 Power tools
Store these in a cupboard, on lipped shelving or on a dedicated worktop.

16 Dust extractor
If possible, make sure that all machines are connected to a dust extractor.

Workbench and accessories

The workbench should be sturdy and level, and at a height that suits you. It offers a flat, supporting surface, and should include at least one vise to hold work securely so that you are free to use tools with both hands. The bench should be heavy enough not to vibrate as you plane or saw; it is often useful to attach it to the floor or a wall.

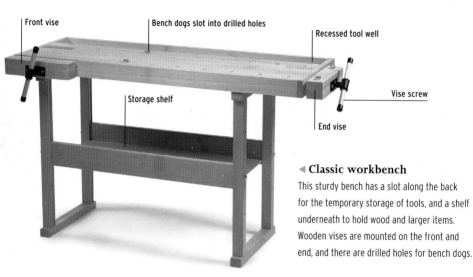

Front vise

Bench dogs slot into drilled holes

Recessed tool well

Storage shelf

Vise screw

End vise

◀ Classic workbench

This sturdy bench has a slot along the back for the temporary storage of tools, and a shelf underneath to hold wood and larger items. Wooden vises are mounted on the front and end, and there are drilled holes for bench dogs.

▶ Portable folding workbench

This bench is useful if space is limited, because it can be folded out of the way when not needed. The worktop is formed from a pair of vise jaws that, together with plastic dogs, can grip or support awkwardly shaped work, including circular sections of large and small diameters. Extra support when sawing or planing can be achieved by placing one foot on the step. However, its lightweight construction means that it is not designed to take a pounding from a mallet. The bench makes a handy platform for temporarily setting up other tools, such as a router table.

Bench dogs slot into drilled holes

Vise jaws

Vise controls

Support step

Vises

▶ 1 Vises are an essential part of the bench for holding work. An integral wooden or metal vise is usually mounted on the front of the bench, with another mounted on the end. They are tightened by rotating a screw. Metal vises should be faced with sturdy scrapwood to prevent the vise from bruising the wood being held (holes to secure a scrapwood facing are almost always predrilled by the manufacturer). As a general rule, keep the wood as low as possible in the vise to avoid chatter (vibration) when sawing or planing.

▼ 2 The two sections of the worktop form the vise on a portable workbench. They have retention grooves for reliable clamping of different materials, such as dowel.

Bench dogs

▼ 1 Bench dogs are plastic, metal or wooden pegs that fit into holes drilled in the bench top to create a stop against which to work. Here, metal bench dogs (with protective scrapwood) are being used to hold an oval workpiece on a classic workbench.

Metal bench dogs

Plastic bench dogs

▼ 2 Plastic bench dogs can be used without protection. Here, an awkward-shaped workpiece is secured with bench dogs on a portable workbench.

Holding and clamping

The need to hold work securely is important. If the wood is not secured, you will not be able to operate tools efficiently and safely. There are also times when just one pair of hands is not enough, and improvised holding devices are needed. As you progress in woodworking, you will probably start to make your own to suit your needs.

C clamp

Holdfast

Bar clamp

Clamps

▼ 1 There are many different types and sizes of clamp available. C clamps are good general-purpose clamps. Place scrapwood between the clamp and workpiece to prevent the clamp from damaging the wood. Some clamps are available with quick-release levers so that you can adjust work quickly.

▲ 2 Bar clamps are useful for long or extra-wide work. Here, square-edged wood is held in a bar clamp and then secured in a vise. The wood can be rotated in the clamp for planing into a circular section.

SEE ALSO
Gluing and clamping,
pages 106–107

▶ 3 Slot the shank of a holdfast into a drilled hole on the bench, and use the tip to hold a workpiece steady.

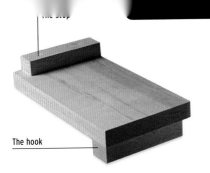

The stop

The hook

▲ ▶ Bench hook

A bench hook is a short board with a batten fixed on the top (the stop) and another on the bottom (the hook) at opposite ends. The hook is placed over the edge of the workbench; the wood being worked is placed against the stop to hold it steady while sawing, planing or chiseling.

Glue gun and sticky tape

■ Use a hot-melt glue gun to hold wood in position temporarily when a vise or clamp might impede the use of tools. Pry the wood loose when you have finished.

■ Double-sided sticky tape is remarkably strong for temporarily securing work to the bench, or for securing jigs to the wood.

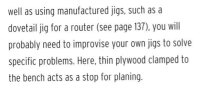

Stops and jigs

▲ 1 These are devices used to hold or guide the wood while it is being worked on, or to hold or guide the tool being used. They help you to carry out a task with greater accuracy, and to repeat that task to make identical pieces. As well as using manufactured jigs, such as a dovetail jig for a router (see page 137), you will probably need to improvise your own jigs to solve specific problems. Here, thin plywood clamped to the bench acts as a stop for planing.

◀ 2 Make a scrapwood jig to guide the saw for cutting dovetail dado joints.

▶ 3 A spindle mounted in a groove is a jig for sanding a circle.

Health and safety

Manufacturers provide full instructions for the safe operation of the tools and equipment they produce; read these carefully before using any item. Take precautions against the dangers that can arise through dust, debris and noise pollution. Minimize the risk of fire by sweeping up dust and chips at the end of the day and disposing of them carefully.

▲ Goggles

Putting on a pair of goggles or a face shield before you start work should become second nature. Eye injuries are the most commonly reported among woodworkers, and you should always wear some form of protection.

▲ Dust mask

Buy the best-quality dust mask that you can find. Some brands are less effective than others, especially if they do not fit snugly around the contour of your nose. Make sure that you choose masks that have a nose clip as an integral part of their design. An all-in-one respirator/face shield provides very good eye and dust protection.

◄ Hearing protectors

Wear earplugs or hearing protectors to protect your hearing from long-term damage whenever you use power and machine tools, such as saws and routers. These soft, padded protectors are inexpensive, and it should soon become a matter of habit to put them on. Noise pollution can also be minimized by insulating individual pieces of equipment.

⚠ Safety guidelines

■ **Workshop environment:** Be neat; this saves time and prevents accidents. Store flammable materials in a cool, safe place, and avoid all skin contact with chemicals and glues. Keep a small first-aid box handy. Install a smoke alarm and fire extinguisher, and dispose of dust and waste regularly to prevent fire. Do not smoke.

■ **Hand tools:** Keep tools sharp, and make cuts away from the body.

■ **Power and machine tools:** Follow the manufacturer's instructions; if in doubt, get some tuition. Tie back long hair, and never wear loose clothing. Beware of trailing cables, unplug machinery before adjusting it, and be sure that all tools are correctly wired and insulated before use. Keep hands well away from moving or cutting edges, and remember that work can be caught by a cutting blade and thrown back at you.

Fit all small power tools, such as a sander, with a dust bag.

▲ ▶ Dust collection

You should limit your exposure to fine wood dust. In broad terms, if you were to puff a heaped teaspoon of dust into the average-sized woodshop and then spend more than 15 minutes a day in this atmosphere, you would be exceeding safe limits. As well as wearing a dust mask or respirator, you should also cut down on the amount of dust at source by using filtered machines and/or by producing shavings rather than dust. Capture as much dust as possible using dust bags and vacuum systems.

Get the largest and most powerful vacuum system you can afford.

◀ Safety guards

When the safety guard is lifted on this drill press, a micro-switch cuts power to the motor.

Modern power and machine tools are equipped with a variety of guards to help protect the operator. Use them as much as possible. If you find a guard difficult to use, call the manufacturer's customer service representative to see if additional help is available. Perhaps you have not installed it properly or it is defective. If you still do not like the guard, check out the various after-market devices. You will see several models demonstrated at most tool shows.

All woodworking tools—both hand tools and powered items—are potentially dangerous. Although guards and other safety devices can be very valuable, they will never replace care and common sense. One of the most definite laws in woodworking is that something can always go wrong.

> ### ⚠ Warning
>
> Many of the safety guards were removed for the photographs in this book to improve clarity. This is not the recommended procedure—safety guards should always be used.

2
Core tools and techniques

How to use the basic hand, power and machine tools

Buying tools

Always buy the best tools you can afford; it is false economy to buy cheap ones. As your skills develop and you undertake more complex projects, the basic toolkit will need to be supplemented with other specialized tools. You will probably also want to invest in some power and machine tools.

Power jigsaw

Hand tools

Most woodworking tools are handheld, but it is those that are operated by the muscles rather than an external power source that are defined as hand tools. When time is pressing, you may prefer to use a powered tool, but there are occasions when it is both quicker and more efficient to use a hand tool—when machines have to be set up, for instance. Using hand tools also helps you to develop a feel for different types of wood, and can be a rewarding and pleasurable experience. The hand tools listed opposite form a woodworker's basic toolkit.

Power tools

Power tools remove the drudgery from such arduous tasks as drilling and chiseling, allowing you to achieve results much more quickly and easily than by hand. They also offer new ways in which wood can be fashioned; the router and biscuit jointer particularly are the power tools that really give the ability to carry out work that would otherwise require a lot of skill and specialized hand tools. A workcenter is a special table to which you can attach various power tools, leaving you with both hands free to maneuver the work—in effect, turning a power tool into a small machine tool. You must always follow all the safety rules when using power tools.

Selection of hand tools

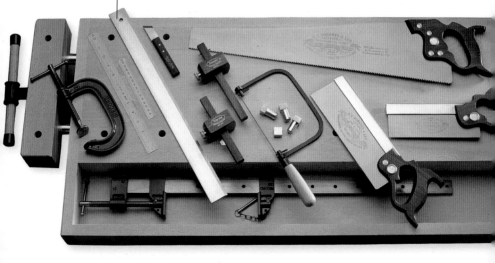

Basic toolkit

■ **Holding and clamping:**
Workbench with vises
Bench dogs
Selection of C clamps
Bar clamps

■ **Measuring and marking:**
Marking knife and awl
Steel rule
Straightedge
Try square
Miter square
Sliding bevel
Marking gauge
Mortise gauge

■ **Sawing:**
General-purpose handsaw
Tenon saw
Dovetail saw
Coping saw

■ **Planing:**
Smoothing plane
or small jack plane
Block plane

■ **Chiseling:**
Bevel-edged chisel
Firmer chisel
Mortise chisel

■ **Drilling and hammering:**
Drill and selection of bits
Mallet
Claw hammer
Pin hammer
Nail set
Selection of screwdrivers

■ **Abrading:**
Sanding block
Sandpaper in various grits

■ **Tool maintenance:**
Oilstone or waterstone

Cordless tools

More and more power tools are now battery rather than electric powered, allowing you the freedom of working without cables. Advances in technology have seen the rates at which battery chargers operate fall from 16 hours to 5 minutes, and some chargers can even diagnose the state of the battery, drain it completely if necessary and recharge all the cells evenly. Some chargers take batteries from a variety of tools.

Battery pack and charger

Machine tools

The availability of small powered machine tools allows you to do precise work at a speed and on a scale that few home woodworkers would have attempted when only hand tools were available. Although combination (or universal) machines are available—which generally include a table saw, spindle molder, jointer planer and sometimes a mortiser and lathe—separate machines are generally more effective and easier to upgrade.

SEE ALSO
Health and safety,
pages 26–27

There are many types and sizes of machine on the market. Always read the owner's manual for your particular tool carefully, paying special attention to safety recommendations. Never be tempted to do a job on your own when you really need someone else to support the work, for safety. If you do not take risks, these tools will save you much time and be a pleasure to use.

Miter
machine saw

Measuring and marking

Accurate measuring and marking are essential; for a piece of cabinetry, for example, accuracy may need to be as fine as $\frac{1}{64}$ in. (0.5mm) or even less. The old adage "measure twice and cut once" is absolutely right. The fact is that huge numbers of mistakes can be avoided or remedied at the measuring and marking stage, before you ever get to cutting the wood. Make sure that the wood is squared (planed so that all sides are at right angles to each other) before measuring and marking joints and component pieces. The most fundamental rule of all in measuring and marking is to check, check and check again.

SEE ALSO
Holding and clamping,
pages 24–25
Planing, pages 62–71
Tool maintenance,
pages 92–99

Basic tools

Effective measuring must be precise. What is crucial, whether you use a steel rule or other measuring aids, is the choice of marker. A basic selection of tools is described here, but there are many different options available.

◄ ▲ Steel rule and tape measure

Use a calibrated steel rule with very clear markings for accurate measuring; 6-, 12- and 24-in. (150, 300 and 600mm) long rules are useful. Use a retractable tape measure for larger measurements, but be aware that it will not be as accurate. The hook at the end of the tape is designed to be loose so that it moves fractionally. The distance it moves should equal the width of the hook; this compensates for the thickness of the hook when taking internal and external measurements, but this can become inaccurate over time.

▲ Choice of marker

The basic markers are a pencil, marking awl and marking knife. As a pencil dulls, its line gets wider and less distinct, so the mark becomes imprecise. An awl mark is consistently narrow, but the line is fuzzy when it is across the grain. A marking knife makes the finest line possible, because it severs the top layer of wood fibers, but when marking along the grain, it can sometimes wander from the rule or straightedge as it follows the grain. As a general rule, use a pencil for guidance marks, and a marking knife (across the grain) or awl (along the grain) for lines that you will saw or chisel.

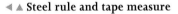

▲ Straightedge

A long straightedge, such as a T-square, is useful for checking that a surface is flat and for marking long lines; a 36-in. (or 1000mm) straightedge is a good size.

Imperial vs. metric

Use *either* imperial *or* metric measures. Never interchange between the two systems. If you try to work the two systems hand-in-hand, you are very likely to make a slip-up that results in the workpiece being cut to the wrong size.

Basic techniques

Use a pencil to make preliminary marks of your measurements, but use a marking knife or awl for final precision marking. Mistakes often occur when two or more pieces have to be marked identically. What usually happens is that small inaccuracies creep in, with the result that all lengths and joints are a poor match. An easy solution is to use measuring or story sticks. Whatever method you use, clear reference marks are essential.

▶ Using a marking knife

A marking knife scores across the wood fibers with a fine line, which provides a good reference point for starting a saw or chisel cut. The blade of the knife is beveled on one side, and should be kept razor sharp. Run the flat side of the blade against a steel rule (or other measuring device). The bevel helps to push the knife tight against the rule as you score the line. Spread your fingers along the rule to make sure that it does not slip. Do not press too hard; aim for a delicate scored line.

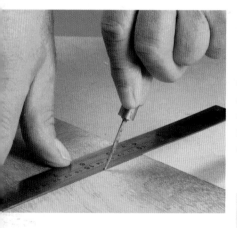

Using an awl

◀ 1 Use an awl to mark a line along the grain. Cup the handle of the awl in the palm of the hand, with the index finger extended along the spike. Place the spike against a steel rule and then draw the awl along its edge. If a rule is not long enough, use a straightedge or T-square. A T-square can easily be made in the workshop; only use it for preliminary marking when cutting large boards roughly down to size, because of accuracy.

▶ 2 You can also use an awl to mark starter holes for drilling, by swiveling the point on the spot.

Measuring and marking curves

◀ 1 Use a compass to mark small circles and arcs. Use it first to "step off" the center mark from adjacent edges. This simply means putting one point against the first edge and roughly marking the center with the other point; then repeat from the adjacent edge. The center of the circle (where you should place the center point of the compass when drawing the circle) is where the two marks intersect.

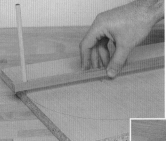

◀ 2 Make a trammel for scribing larger curves. Drill a hole at one end of a narrow piece of wood to take a pencil; use a brad as the center point at the required distance.

▶ 3 Finding the center of circular pieces of wood, such as turnery blanks, can be achieved using a workshop-made center square. This has two arms at 90 degrees to one another, with a third central arm at 45 degrees. With the center square positioned at two points around the circle, make pencil marks roughly in the center. The center of the circle is where the two marks intersect.

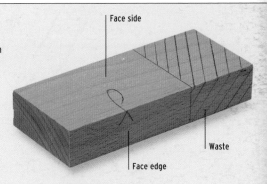

Reference marks

A lot of woodworking mistakes have to do with mixing up the various faces of the wood, so identify the parts with pencil marks. The face (best) side should be marked with a loop that trails off toward the face (best) edge, which should be marked with an arrow connecting to the loop. Make all your measurements from these marked points of reference. Areas of wood to be cut away as waste should be shaded clearly.

Face side

Waste

Face edge

Measuring sticks

▶ **1** A measuring stick is any flat, straight piece of wood that can act as a template. Mark the required measurement onto the stick, or cut it to the required size, then transfer the measurement from the stick onto the main wood as many times as necessary.

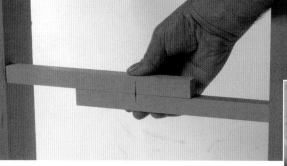

Measuring stick

◀ **2** Use a pair of measuring sticks to measure an internal length. Place a mark across the sticks where they overlap.

▶ **3** Use the overlapping sticks to mark the required length onto other components.

◀ Story sticks

A story stick is a more complex version of a measuring stick. All the component pieces of a project are measured and marked onto the stick, including all necessary details and notes. Each project will probably require a story stick for its vertical and horizontal planes, either on separate sticks or the back and front of a single stick.

Calipers

▶ 1 Calipers are ideal for making precise internal, external and depth measurements. Digital calipers, which display the measurements on a screen, are the easiest to use; they can be set to either imperial or metric mode.

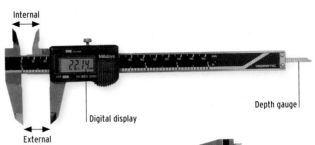

Internal

External

Digital display

Depth gauge

▲ 2 Use the external arms to measure a tenon.

▲ 3 Use the internal arms to measure a mortise.

▲ 4 Use the depth gauge to set the height of a table saw blade.

Triangle marking

Triangle marking is a method of coding pieces of work so that they can be reassembled in the correct order later. It is especially useful when there are numerous and sometimes duplicate parts, such as a set of drawers. Simply draw a triangle on the faces of each set of components; the triangles should point up or away from the viewer. Use underscores to distinguish each set of duplicate parts.

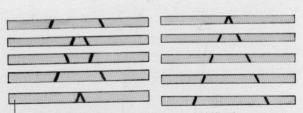

Boards for a tabletop in the wrong (left) and correct (right) order.

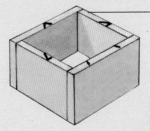

Place opposite drawer sides together and mark with triangles.

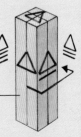

Triangles with underscores indicate the faces of table legs.

Marking with squares

Squares are used to mark lines at a precise angle to a reference edge, as well as to check the angles of component pieces. Use a try square for 90-degree angles, a miter square for 45-degree angles and a sliding bevel for any other angle. All are available with different blade lengths.

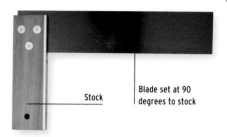

Stock

Blade set at 90 degrees to stock

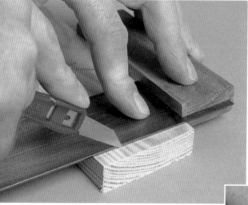

◄ ▲ Try square

Measure along the edge of the wood and mark the point where you want the 90-degree line to be. Place the tip of a marking knife at this point, then move the blade of the square up to the knife. Squeeze the stock of the square firmly against the edge of the wood, then carefully mark a line tight against the blade. To achieve a perfectly square cut, use the try square to extend the line all the way around the wood.

Checking a try square

A try square can become inaccurate if it is mishandled or dropped. To test that it is set at precisely 90 degrees, first set it down on a length of planed, straight-edged wood so that the stock butts hard up against the edge. Draw a line along the blade with a ballpoint pen. Flip the square over, keeping it butted to the same edge. If the blade still aligns with the drawn line, then it is accurate.

▲ Repeat accuracy

To mark several identical pieces, you can simply clamp them together and square the marks across all the pieces in one go using a try square.

◀ ▶ Miter square

Use a miter square in the same way as a try square for marking lines at 45 degrees to a reference edge. Here, both tools are used to mark alternately all the way around the wood to mark a miter joint.

Blade set at 45 degrees to stock

▶ Sliding bevel

A sliding bevel can be adjusted to any angle. As with a try square, the stock should be held firmly against the edge of the wood.

Tighten wingnut to secure blade at any angle

◀ ▶ Combination square

A combination square combines a try square, miter square and steel rule. It is usually not as accurate as dedicated squares, and is heavier and more cumbersome, but can be very useful.

Adjustable steel rule

Use this side of stock for 45-degree angles

Saw thickness

When two or more pieces are to be cut from the same board, remember to mark spacing lines to allow for the saw cut. Be aware that the groove the saw cuts (the kerf) is fractionally wider than the thickness of the saw. Mark the lines across both the face side and edge, to help you guide the saw blade.

Spacing lines for saw kerf

Use this side of stock for 90-degree angles

Marking with gauges

Use a gauge to mark a line parallel to a reference edge. The standard marking gauge is composed of a beam with a small steel pin protruding from it. The beam slides through a hole in a block of wood, called the stock. The stock is secured to the beam with a thumbscrew.

Steel pin scribes the line

Stock moves along beam

Beam

Thumbscrew secures stock in position

▲ ▶ Marking gauge

Use a steel rule to measure the required distance between the pin and the stock—that is, the distance you want the parallel line to be from the edge of the wood. Adjust the position of the stock and screw in place. Recheck the position of the stock, tapping the ends of the beam against the bench to finetune it if necessary. Hold the stock firmly against the edge of the wood, with the pin toward you, then push the gauge away from you so that the pin lightly scores the wood. It is better to use several light passes, rather than a single heavy pass.

Chalk line

You cannot use a gauge to mark a straight line on a board that is waney-edged. Stretch a length of chalked string taut along the board, then pluck it so that it marks a straight chalk line onto the board.

▼ Cutting gauge

A cutting gauge has a beveled blade like that of a marking knife instead of a pin. It is good for crossgrain scoring and cutting veneer.

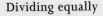

Extra pin for
standard marking

Controls for adjusting
movable mortise pin

Steel pins for marking
mortises (one fixed,
one movable)

▲ ▶ Mortise gauge

A mortise gauge has two metal pins
on the beam. By setting the pins to
a certain width apart and at a certain
distance from the stock, you can
draw both lines needed to cut a
mortise or tenon. Make sure that
you draw the lines of the tenon
and mortise components from
the same reference edge.

Dividing equally

This example demonstrates
how to divide a board into
four equal widths, but the
same principle can be
applied to any number of
divisions. Lay a steel rule at
an angle across the board,
so that 0 is at one edge and
a measurement that is easily
divisible by 4 is at the other
edge—here, 16. Mark the
board at the 4, 8 and 12
divisions on the rule, then
use a marking gauge to mark
parallel lines along the board
at each of these divisions.

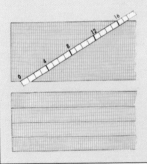

◀ ▼ Improvised gauges

Place a pencil or marking knife
against the end of a combination
square blade, then draw them along
the edge of the wood. When absolute
precision is not necessary, you can
run your fingers along the edge of
the wood and mark with a pencil.

▶ Profile gauge

Use a profile gauge to copy
a shape and act as a template. Push
the gauge against the shape to record
the outline, then trace it onto the wood.

Sawing

The saw is one of the oldest tools, and its action is very simple.
A series of teeth are set outward in alternate directions along a
flat steel blade and sharpened to an angle; the angle is determined
by the type of work the saw has to do. The more teeth per inch (tpi),
the finer the cut. The groove that the saw cuts, called the kerf, is
fractionally wider than the thickness of the saw in order to give
clearance. Accurate hand sawing takes a lot of practice, and it calls
for precision on your part, not force. There are also power and
machine saws available that cut smoothly, accurately and quickly.
Choose your tools according to personal preference and the type
of work you are most likely to do.

SEE ALSO

Holding and clamping,
pages 24–25

Measuring and marking,
pages 32–41

Tool maintenance,
pages 92–99

Types of saw cut

A square cut is when the wood is sawn at 90 degrees to adjacent faces and edges, but wood can also be sawn at other angles to create miters and bevels. Some saws are used to shape the wood with curves. The grooves, dadoes and rabbets that form the basis of many joints can also be cut with different types of saw.

▶ **Ripping and crosscutting**
Cutting along the grain is known as ripping or ripsawing. Cutting across the grain is known as crosscutting.

▶ **Cutting angles**
A miter is created by cutting the wood at an angle of 45 degrees; any angle other than 45 or 90 degrees creates a bevel. When wood is cut at an angle on two different planes, it is a compound angle.

▼ **Groove, dado and rabbet**
A channel cut into the wood is known as a groove when it is along the grain or a dado when it is across the grain. Grooves and dadoes can be cut in a variety of ways, such as by using a backsaw to cut the edges of the channel and then chiseling out the waste, or entirely by machine sawing. A wide dado is sometimes called a trench; a deep dado is sometimes called a notch. A stepped recess cut at the end or edge of a piece of wood is called a rabbet.

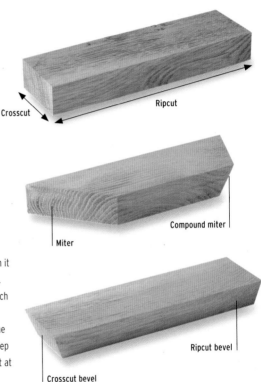

Crosscut

Ripcut

Compound miter

Miter

Ripcut bevel

Crosscut bevel

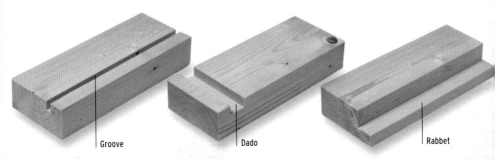

Groove

Dado

Rabbet

Choosing a saw

All types of saw cut can be achieved with hand tools. A general-purpose handsaw, a couple of backsaws in different sizes and a frame saw would form a good basic sawing kit. If you wish to use power or machine saws, use the chart below to help you make suitable choices.

Type of saw	Pros	Cons
Scroll saw (page 49)	Intricately shaped, tightly angled, curved and internal cuts	Only suitable for smallscale work
Jigsaw (page 50)	Curved, straight, angled and internal cuts; can be used freehand; cordless available	Not as accurate as a machine saw for straight and angled cuts
Portable circular saw (page 51)	Straight and angled cuts; cordless available	Not as accurate as a machine saw
Table saw (pages 52–55)	Ideal for ripping; can also crosscut and do miters, bevels, compound angles, grooves, dadoes and rabbets; fast, powerful and accurate	Caution required, because of risk of kickback; needs clearance all around, so takes up lots of space; crosscuts limited by size of table (but sliding table attachments can increase this)
Miter saw (pages 56–57)	Extremely accurate cross-, miter, bevel and compound-angle cuts; can also do dadoes and rabbets; quick to set up; portable	Cannot ripcut
Radial-arm saw (pages 58–59)	Excels at crosscutting; can also do ripcuts, miters, bevels, compound angles, grooves, dadoes and rabbets; can be placed against a wall; accessories are available for other tasks	Great caution required, because blade is exposed and moving; limited by arm length, so awkward for ripping wide boards
Bandsaw (pages 60–61)	Ideal for curves; can also do cross- and ripcuts, miters, bevels, compound angles and rabbets; relatively quiet and safe—the blade thrusts downward; can cut thick wood	Does not cut as cleanly or as fast as other machine saws on straight cuts

◀ ▶ Saw blades

Saw blades are designed for a variety of jobs, from ripping to crosscutting to general-purpose; some also give a very smooth finish. Some blades are disposed of when blunt, such as jigsaw blades, while others can be resharpened, such as circular saw blades. It is always worth buying circular saw blades with tungsten-carbide tips. They are more expensive and need to be professionally sharpened, but they easily prove their worth in their cutting abilities and duration of service.

Jigsaw blades

▶ Machine saw safety

Use tools to feed the wood into a machine saw and keep your hands away from the blade. A pushstick is a strip of hardwood or plywood with a notch at one end for pushing the workpiece; the stick is rounded at the other end for holding. A featherboard has a series of saw kerfs at one end, creating a springlike action to keep the stock from wandering as you guide it through the machine.

▲ Laser guides

Many power and machine saws, such as the jigsaw and miter saw, are available with laser guides; if not, you can buy a laser guide and fit it to your tool. The laser emits a narrow red beam along the path of the blade; some emit two closely spaced beams to indicate the saw kerf.

Handsawing tips

■ Align the blade so that the cut is entirely on the waste side of the cutting line; otherwise, the thickness of the blade will be deducted from the dimensions of the piece you are cutting.

■ Tearout is caused when a blade tears out (rather than cuts) the wood fibers as it exits a cut. Try to orient cuts so that any tearout will be on the unexposed sides of projects.

■ Do not saw too close to the edge of the wood, because this can cause fibers to disintegrate—¼ in. (6mm) should be the minimum distance.

■ Always support the waste wood as you near the end of a cut so that it does not break off and splinter.

Handsaw

Handsaws are used for cutting wood and manmade boards into smaller components. They are differentiated by the number and angle of the saw teeth, depending on whether they are designed to cut along or across the grain. Ripsaws are for cutting along the grain; crosscut saws are for cutting across the grain; general-purpose panel saws can be used for both. All types are available in a range of blade lengths.

General-purpose panel saw

Using a handsaw

◄ **1** Clamp the wood to a workbench or support it lower on a sawhorse or any firm base; you may need to use a knee to hold the wood steady. Grip the saw handle firmly, with the index finger pointing forward to give greater control. Place the blade at an angle against the far corner, on the waste side of the marked cutting line.

▲ **2** Make a few short backward strokes to establish the cut. Use your thumb to guide the blade's path.

► **3** Switch to long, steady strokes back and forth to complete the cut. Keep your eye directly above and in line with the blade for accuracy. A good saw should cut smoothly almost under its own weight; your task is to guide the saw, not to press it down. If everything feels and sounds really rough, you are probably using the saw at the wrong angle. Wedge a small piece of wood in the kerf if it begins to close up on the blade.

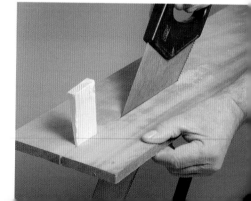

Backsaw

Backsaws have a strip of steel or brass along the back of the blade for stiffening, giving better control than a handsaw. They also have a greater number of finer teeth, for a cleaner and more accurate cut. Use them for trimming pieces and cutting joints. A tenon saw is the best general-purpose backsaw; it derives its name from cutting tenons. A dovetail saw is a miniature tenon saw; it is used for fine work as well as for dovetails.

Tenon saw

Dovetail saw

Using a backsaw

◄ **1** Secure the wood; a bench hook is used here. Align the marked cutting line with the end (stop) of the bench hook. Grip the saw handle firmly, with the index finger extended for extra control. Use your other hand to hold the wood against the stop of the bench hook. Working on the waste side of the line, draw the saw gently back across the far corner against the end of the hook a few times to start the cut. Keep your eye above and in line with the blade.

▶ **2** Once the cut is established, move the saw parallel to the surface and cut back along the whole cutting line to start a saw channel. Then switch to smooth back and forth strokes to complete the cut.

▼ **3** Alternatively, secure the wood in a vise and use a two-handed grip to saw the wood. This makes it easier to follow the marked cutting line.

Frame saw

Frame saws consist of a narrow blade held in a frame. Whereas a hand- or backsaw can only cut straight into the wood, the blade of a frame saw can be swiveled so that you can cut in any direction. Use the saw for cutting very fine lines and curves. A coping saw is a good general-purpose frame saw; it is especially useful for removing waste from dovetails where a backsaw would be too large.

Coping saw

Blade slots onto retaining pins at each end of frame

Turn handle to tighten or loosen frame for adjusting blade

Using a coping saw

◄ 1 Secure the wood in a vise so that both hands are free for extra control. If cutting an internal shape, first drill an access hole in the wood just inside the marked cutting line. Loosen the handle of the saw and unclip one end of the blade from the retaining pin. Thread the blade through the drilled hole. Push the frame against your hip to flex it slightly, then slot the blade back into the retaining pin. Tighten the handle to tension the blade; make sure that the retaining pins at each end of the blade align so that the blade is not twisted.

▶ 2 Hold the saw with both hands, and use back and forth strokes to cut along the waste side of the line. The blade can be rotated in the frame so that the saw will cut in any desired path; twist the handle to loosen or tighten the blade for making adjustments. Unclip one end of the blade to remove the saw when you have finished.

Scroll saw

Also known as a powered fretsaw, the scroll saw is a fine-toothed saw with an inexpensive, disposable blade that cuts with a rapid up and down motion. It is used for cutting tight angles and all manner of curves and intricate shapes. The table can also be tilted for cutting bevels. The saw should be attached to a workbench or special stand.

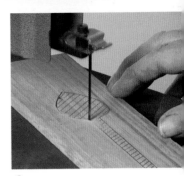

▲ **2** Hold the wood firmly down on the table and feed it steadily into the blade. Keep your hands to either side of the blade, never directly in line with it. Slow down at tight curves and angles to allow the blade to clear space around itself, then change the direction of the cut.

Using a scroll saw

◀ **1** Refer to the manufacturer's instructions to choose the correct blade size for the thickness of material you are cutting. To make an enclosed cut, remove the blade from the saw by slackening the tension adjuster. Drill a hole in the waste area, then feed the blade through the hole. Reattach the blade to the saw.

▲ **3** To cut a bevel, tilt the table to the required angle, then cut in the normal way.

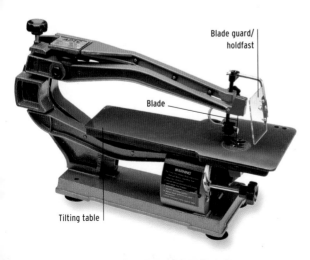

Blade guard/holdfast

Blade

Tilting table

Blade guard/holdfast

The blade guard can swivel around to act as a holdfast. This is useful for holding down thin workpieces so that they do not vibrate.

Jigsaw

The jigsaw is a versatile tool for making straight, curved or angled cuts. Most jigsaws have variable speed and both reciprocating (up and down) and adjustable orbital (back and forth) action for a more efficient cut. A jigsaw is easy to operate once you learn to keep the pressure against the surface of the wood to counteract the upward snatching of the blade (caused by the teeth of the blade facing upward).

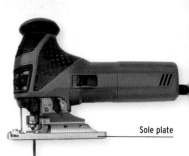

Sole plate

◄ Jigsaw blades

Jigsaw blades are disposable and easy to change. They are available for use with different materials and in a range of lengths.

Using a jigsaw

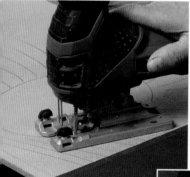

◄ **1** When cutting curves, align the blade with the cutting line, switch on and follow the line freehand. For tight curves, saw straight cuts through the waste wood up to the curve, then cut along the curved line.

▲ **3** For straight cuts, guide the jigsaw alongside a clamped batten or use the side fence that comes with the tool. You can tilt the sole plate to make angled cuts.

► **2** For internal cuts, either drill an access hole to insert the blade or use a plunge-cutting technique using a special blade. To do this, tilt the jigsaw onto the front of the sole plate, switch on, then pivot the jigsaw upright so that the blade cuts into the wood.

► **4** Improvise a trammel for cutting circles, using the slots in the sole plate designed for attaching a side fence.

Portable circular saw

This handy tool is used for making straight cuts. Different blades are available for cutting along or across the grain. They come in various diameters, and can be set to full or part depth by lowering or raising the sole plate, so that you can cut completely or partially through the wood. The sole plate can also be adjusted to cut at an angle of up to 45 degrees.

Dust-extraction port

Fixed blade guard

Pivoting blade guard

Riving knife

Sole plate

Blade

Using a circular saw

◀ **1** Clamp the workpiece securely and use the alignment notch at the front of the sole plate to position the saw. Use both hands firmly on the handles to control the saw, and start the motor before the blade engages with the wood.

Riving knife

A riving knife is a curved metal strip mounted behind the saw blade. It prevents the kerf (saw cut) from closing up around the blade and causing a jam that could be dangerous.

▶ **2** To make a cut parallel to the edge of the wood, mount the side fence onto the sole plate and adjust it to the required distance. Keep the fence tight against the edge while you saw. Use a clamped batten as a guide for cutting the wood at other positions.

▼ **3** Adjust the angle of the sole plate to make an angled cut.

Table saw

The table saw consists of a metal table with an opening in the center through which a circular saw blade protrudes. The blade can be raised, lowered or tilted up to 45 degrees. The table saw is used for making quick and accurate straight cuts along and across the grain; it will also cut grooves, dadoes and rabbets. A tungsten-carbide tipped combination (or universal) blade is a good general-purpose choice.

Miter fence

The miter fence runs in slots milled into the table on each side of the blade opening. The fence supports the wood as it is crosscut on the saw, and can be angled for miters and bevels. For long pieces of work, you may find it helpful to attach a scrapwood extension to the miter fence; some table saws can be fitted with an adjustable sliding carriage for crosscutting large materials.

Blade guard

All table saws come with some form of blade guard; it is essential that you use it. Note that the guard has been removed in some of the photographs for clarity.

Rip fence

The rectangular rip fence sits parallel to the blade. When you rip a piece of wood (cut along its length), the fence guides the wood as it is being pushed across the blade. Never try to do this, or any other, operation freehand on the saw; the chances that you will lose control are too great.

Table extension

Blade-height control

For the cleanest cut, set the blade so that the teeth protrude above the workpiece by about 1/4 in. (6mm). This is also a safety precaution—do not expose any more blade than necessary.

Blade-angle control

You can tilt the blade up to 45 degrees.

Ripsawing

▼ 1 To cut along the grain, adjust the rip fence to the correct distance from the blade. If cutting a wide board, keep your hands well away from the blade as you guide the wood along the table and against the fence. For narrower workpieces, use a pushstick and featherboard to guide the wood so that your fingers are kept well clear of the blade.

▶ 2 To ripsaw a waney-edged board, pin a slightly larger sheet of plywood to the bottom of the board. You can then guide the plywood along the rip fence to remove the waney edges.

Note: The blade guard has been removed from all photographs on this page for clarity only. A blade guard must be used for these techniques.

⚠ Kickback safety

■ Kickback is always a danger when using a table saw, and you cannot rely on the riving knife (see page 51) to prevent it. Always stand to the side, never directly behind, the blade, so that if any wood does get kicked back toward you, you will be safe.

■ Another protection is to adjust the rip fence so that it is skewed just a whisker at the end behind the blade. This offset makes is easier for the wood to pass off the saw after being cut. Wood only needs to contact the fence before the cut. Alternatively, clamp a block of scrapwood to the fence so that there is space for the wood to move after passing the blade.

▼ Crosscutting

To cut across the grain, set the miter fence at 90 degrees to the blade. For long pieces, attach an extension batten to the miter fence. Use both hands to grip the wood against the fence, and also to push the fence along its slot to feed the wood across the blade; clamp the workpiece to the fence if it helps. As a guide for making repeat cuts, you can clamp a block of scrapwood to the rip fence (right) or extension batten (below) to act as a stop.

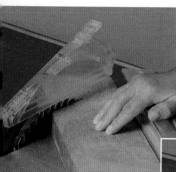

Cutting angles

◀ **1** Angle the sliding miter fence to 45 degrees for a miter cut. You can position the miter fence at other angles to cut bevels at various angles.

▶ **2** You can cut a miter on a different plane of the wood by keeping the miter fence at 90 degrees to the blade but tilting the blade to 45 degrees.

▲ **3** If you angle both the miter fence and the blade to 45 degrees, you will create a compound miter cut.

Cutting a rabbet or tongue

◀ **1** Refer to the box opposite regarding special blade guards for this technique. It is best to cut the narrowest edge of the wood first. Set the rip fence the required distance from the blade and make the first cut for the rabbet. If cutting a tongue, as here, turn the wood around and make a second cut on the other side.

▶ **2** Reposition the rip fence and sever the waste on one side to form a rabbet. Cut another rabbet on the other side to form a tongue.

⚠ Safety

When you turn the wood to make the second cut of a rabbet, make sure that you position the wood so that the waste is not trapped against the fence, because this could cause kickback.

Cutting a groove

▶ **1** Refer to the box below regarding special blade guards for this technique. Lower the saw blade so that it will only cut through the wood to the required depth of groove. Set the rip fence the required distance from the blade, and guide the wood along the rip fence to make a cut for the first side of the groove. Repeat to make a cut for the other side of the groove.

▶ **2** Remove the waste from the groove with multiple passes over the saw blade, adjusting the rip fence so that you achieve a series of tightly spaced saw cuts across the groove. Continue until all the waste is removed.

⚠ Safety guards

■ The standard blade guard cannot be used when cutting grooves, rabbets or tongues on a table saw. Special guards are available that hold down the work and form a kind of tunnel that surrounds the work as it passes across the blade. This guard is not shown in the photographs on these two pages because it obscures the techniques being demonstrated, but it is essential that you use one.

■ When using special cutters, such as a dado set, you need to fit a special protective throat plate around the blade opening.

▼ Cutting a dado

You can cut a dado in the same way as a groove. However, if you need to cut a lot of dadoes, it may be worthwhile buying a special set of blades, called a dado set. The set comprises two outer blades for cutting the sides of the dado, with chipper blades between them for

removing the waste and smoothing the base of the dado. Adjust the width of the dado set by adding or removing some of the chipper blades until you achieve the required width. Once the set is mounted on the saw, you can cut a dado in a single pass.

Miter saw

Also known as a chop saw or drop saw, the miter saw is a type of overhead circular saw that makes extremely accurate crosscuts, miters and bevels. This portable machine consists of a circular saw blade suspended above a rotating table; the table and blade can be swiveled to 45 degrees for cutting miters. The blades of compound miter saws can also be tilted for cutting bevels and compound angles. On a sliding miter saw, the blade can be pulled along a sliding arm toward you, which increases the saw's cutting capacity to include wide materials.

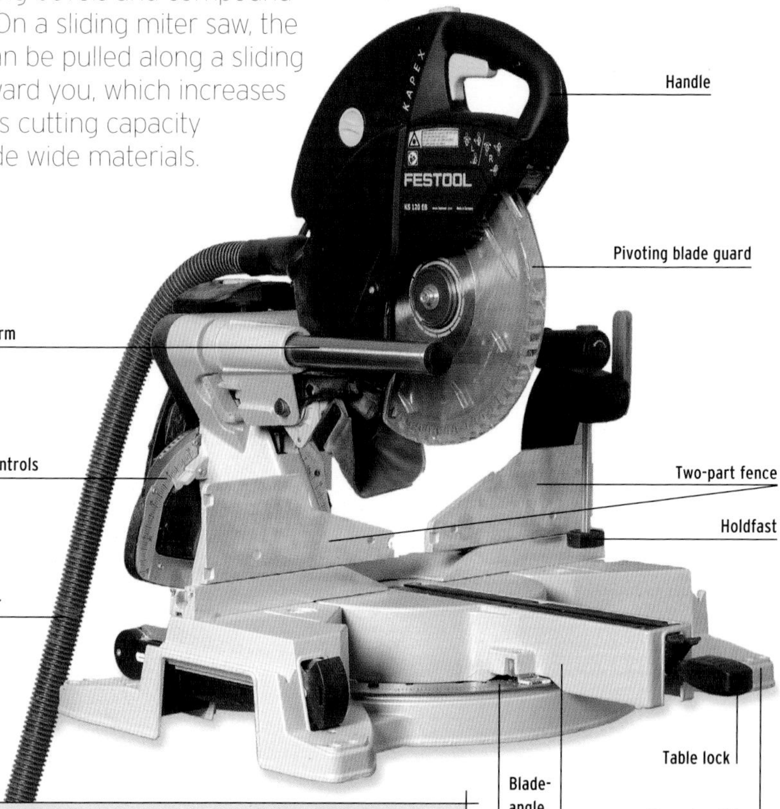

Handle

Pivoting blade guard

Sliding arm

Blade-tilt controls

Two-part fence

Holdfast

Dust extractor

Table lock

Blade-angle scale

Base should be bolted securely to workbench when using the saw

Flipover saw

This portable machine does the work of both a miter saw and a table saw. It consists of a circular saw attached to a folding table base. The saw can be used above the table like a miter saw, or flipped over so that the blade is under the table and protrudes through it to do the job of a table saw.

Rotating table; some have extension arms for supporting long workpieces

▶ Crosscutting

With the blade at 90 degrees to the fence, hold the wood against the fence, with the cutting line aligned with the blade. Switch on the saw, and use the handle to lower the blade and push it forward toward the fence to make the cut; the blade guard will retract automatically. When you lift the blade after making the cut, the guard will lower. To cut a wide board with a sliding miter saw, simply pull the blade toward you along the sliding arm, switch on the motor and then make the cut.

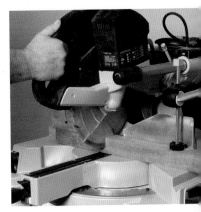

Cutting angles

◀ **1** To cut a miter, rotate the table to the 45-degree mark. Position the wood against the fence and make the cut in the usual way. Alter the angle of the table to cut bevels.

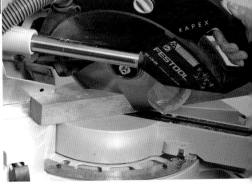

▶ **2** For a compound cut, rotate the table and tilt the blade at the same time. If you set both to 45 degreees, you will cut a compound miter. You may need to adjust the position of the fence to allow more clearance for the blade; check by lowering the blade with the power off.

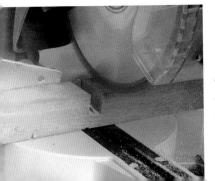

◀ Dadoes and rabbets

With some miter saws, you can adjust the depth of cut. This allows you to cut the two shoulder lines for each side of a dado; you can then remove the waste between them with a series of tightly spaced saw cuts. Use the same procedure for cutting a rabbet.

Radial-arm saw

The radial-arm saw is an overhead circular saw suspended from a horizontal arm that swings from side to side. The blade can be moved to any position along the arm. The saw is primarily used for crosscutting, but is also capable of ripsawing. The blade can be rotated and tilted for cutting miters, bevels and compound angles, and also raised or lowered to adjust the depth of cut for grooves, dadoes and rabbets.

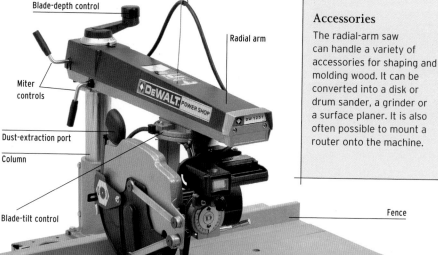

Blade-depth control

Radial arm

Miter controls

Dust-extraction port

Column

Blade-tilt control

Fence

Accessories

The radial-arm saw can handle a variety of accessories for shaping and molding wood. It can be converted into a disk or drum sander, a grinder or a surface planer. It is also often possible to mount a router onto the machine.

Table

When cutting through a piece of wood completely, the blade of a radial-arm saw has to cut into the table on which the wood rests. Protect the table by attaching a thin sheet of MDF or plywood with double-sided adhesive tape. Replace the board as necessary.

Blade guard and anti-kickback device

When you start a cut, the blade guard automatically retracts to expose just enough of the blade to make the required depth of cut; it automatically encloses the blade afterward. During ripsawing, you should lower the riving knife behind the blade to keep the kerf clear and activate the anti-kickback device to prevent work from being thrown back toward you.

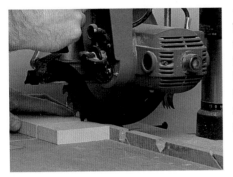

◀ Crosscutting

With the blade locked at 90 degrees to the fence, hold the wood against the fence, with the cutting line aligned with the blade. You may find it helpful to cut notches in the fence as reference points for alignment. You can clamp a stop to the fence when cutting several pieces to the same dimensions. Pull the saw blade across the wood; it will return to its original position automatically afterward.

▶ Ripsawing

Set up the riving knife and anti-kickback device (refer to the manufacturer's instructions). Rotate the blade by 90 degrees so that it is parallel to the fence, and lock in position. Use pushsticks to feed the wood under the blade. Feed it in the opposite direction from the rotation of the blade; if you do it the other way, the blade may snatch the wood from your hands.

▼ Cutting a rabbet, groove or dado

Adjust the depth of cut, then pull the saw head across in a series of tightly spaced cuts. Knock the wood against a bench top so that the the sawn strips snap off, then use the saw to make the surface perfectly level. The same procedure can be used for cutting grooves and dadoes (or use a dado set instead; see page 55).

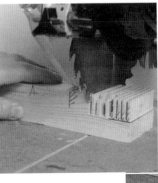

▲ Cutting angles

To cut a miter, swing the arm to 45 degrees and lock in position. Place the wood against the fence, align correctly, then pull the radial arm toward you to make a crosscut. Bevels can be crosscut or ripsawn; simply tilt the blade to the required angle.

Bandsaw

This general-purpose saw has a narrow continuous-loop blade running around either two or three wheels, one of which is electrically driven. This flexible blade is suitable for cutting curves and straight lines, and the table can be tilted up to 45 degrees for cutting miters and bevels. The downward thrust of the blade means that there is no danger of kickback.

Blade guard and guides

These should be lowered to permit just sufficient clearance of the workpiece under them—about $\frac{1}{2}$–1 in. (15–25mm). Adjust the blade guides so that they support the back and sides of the exposed blade. There should be a slight clearance at the back edge of the blade, and the blade should be central between the runners of the guides. Note that they are not shown in the recommended position in some of the photographs opposite so that the path of the blade can be seen more clearly. Refer to the manufacturer's instructions for setting them correctly.

Throat capacity

The throat capacity (distance between blade and vertical column) determines the maximum width of cut. The distance between the table and raised blade guides determines the maximum thickness of wood that can be cut.

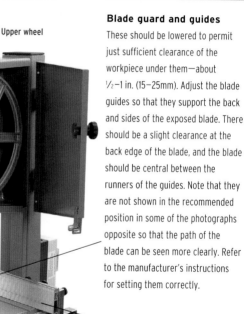

Upper wheel

Rip fence

Slot for miter fence

Tilting table

Lower wheel housing

Blade

Many different saw blades are available, designed for cutting different materials. There are also blades with larger teeth for fast cutting or finer teeth for a fine finish, plus narrow blades for cutting tight curves. Tension the blade as instructed in the manual.

Cutting curves

▶ 1 Place the wood on the table and feed it freehand through the machine, following the marked curve and keeping your hands clear of the blade. If the blade begins to bind in a tight curve, simply allow it to run out through the waste to the side of the piece. Then begin again, cutting a series of shallow curves until you complete the required shape.

▶ 2 In situations where you cannot run the blade out through the waste, make a series of straight cuts up to the marked curve, then cut the curve. The waste wood will fall away.

◀ Ripsawing

With the workpiece against the rip fence, adjust the fence to align the marked cutting line with the blade. Feed the wood through the machine, keeping it pressed against the fence. As you near the end of the cut, use a pushstick and featherboard to feed the wood through.

▼ Crosscutting

Fit the sliding miter fence onto the table and place the workpiece against it so that the cutting line aligns with the blade. If you need to cut several identical pieces, attach an extension batten to the miter fence and clamp a block of scrapwood to it to act as a stop. Slide the fence along the table to make the cut.

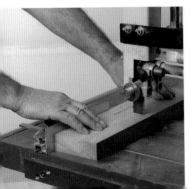

Cutting angles and rabbets

■ Angle the miter fence to cut miters. Tilt the table to cut a bevel. If you combine a tilted table with an angled miter fence, you will create a compound cut.

■ Cut the rabbets for a tenon by crosscutting the shoulder lines, then ripsawing away the waste. Some bandsaws have depth stops, but clamped blocks of scrapwood can be used as stops instead.

Planing

There is hardly any woodworking that does not include planing somewhere in its process, whether it be smoothing a surface flat, trimming joints true or shaping a piece of wood to a given dimension. Machine planing is quick and highly accurate, but mastering the basics of hand planing will give you more versatility and a better understanding of the character of wood. By hand planing, you come to understand how the blade cuts and how different woods and grain directions affect the finish. Even the best job of planing will leave slight ridges on the surface; these can be removed by abrading with a sander if desired.

SEE ALSO

Holding and clamping,
pages 24–25

Measuring and marking,
pages 32–41

Abrading,
pages 86–91

Tool maintenance,
pages 92–99

Hand planes

Bench planes, such as a smoothing or jack plane, are used to smooth the surface of the wood until it is perfectly flat, and to square the edges. A small block plane is useful for fine work, particularly trimming end grain, and a spokeshave for curved workpieces.

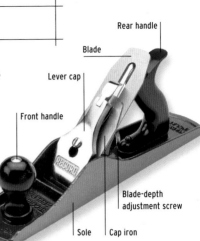

Rear handle

Blade

Lever cap

Front handle

Blade-depth adjustment screw

Sole | Cap iron

▶ Smoothing plane

Shorter than a jack plane, the smoothing plane, with its fine blade adjustments, is used to take very fine shavings to produce a smooth surface before finishing.

▲ Jack plane

The jack plane, or fore plane, is a good general-purpose plane that can be used for rough smoothing, joining or final smoothing.

▶ Block plane

The small block plane has a shallower blade angle than other bench planes and is used for delicate work, such as trimming end grain, planing bevels and smoothing narrow edges.

▼ Spokeshave

A spokeshave is essentially a miniature hand plane. It is used for accurate shaping and smoothing, especially curves. Spokeshaves can have a flat sole for working on flat or convex surfaces, or a rounded role for concave surfaces.

Size of bench plane

Bench planes come in a range of sizes. A long bench plane gives a more accurate result, because it rides over high spots on the wood, gradually removing them until the wood is even and a single long shaving can be taken off. A smaller plane follows the contours of the surface. For the beginner, the best compromise is a plane that is heavy enough to avoid chatter (vibration when the blade does not fully engage with the wood fibers due to lightness), but not so long and heavy as to be cumbersome. A smoothing or small jack plane would be ideal.

Hand planing

The plane blade must be razor sharp and carefully adjusted to take shavings of the depth required. If the cut is too thick, you will have less control of the plane. Adjust the depth of the blade whenever necessary throughout the planing process to give a controlled cut. Try to plane in the direction of the grain; for irregular grain, set the plane for the finest cut possible and work slowly.

Planing surfaces

▶ **1** Hold the board on the workbench, against a bench stop or in a vise for small pieces. Hold the rear handle of the bench plane with one hand; extend your forefinger for greater control. Hold the front handle with your other hand to keep the front of the plane in contact with the wood. Stand with shoulder, hip and plane in line for full control, feet slightly apart. Keep the plane close to your body for extra control, and push the plane by swaying forward at your knees rather than extending your arms. Aim to plane the wood with a smooth motion across the whole board.

▼ **2** Alter the downward pressure from front to back handle over the course of the stroke. The transfer of pressure will stop the plane from rounding the work at the ends of the wood. Do not lift the plane off the wood until the blade is beyond the end of the board.

Beginning of stroke

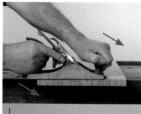

Middle of stroke

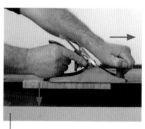

End of stroke

▲ Slicing irregular grain

Planing wood with irregular grain can be difficult. For the initial cuts, hold the plane at about a 45-degree angle to the edge of the board, but push it straight up the board. As the surface becomes smoother, reduce the angle until it is parallel to the edge.

▼ Planing wide boards

Wide boards, or boards that have been joined together, can be planed across the grain to remove stock quickly. This is because fibers are weak across the grain and easily severed. Finish by planing with the grain.

Planing test

Using a pencil or ballpoint pen, mark three equidistant lines across the wood, and number equal intervals at the end of the wood (here, 1 to 6). The idea is to plane off in one cut all three lines at position 1 and work progressively across the work to position 6. The center of the plane should be lined up with each number. Check the lines to see whether you are applying pressure consistently from the beginning to the end of each cut.

Planing edges

▶ 1 Mount the wood in a vise. To keep the plane centered on a narrow edge, put your thumb on top near the front handle and run your fingers along the side of the wood to guide the plane. Use a try square to check that the edge is at 90 degrees.

▶ 2 To plane a beveled edge, tilt the wood in the vise so that the planing is done horizontally. The force of gravity helps with downward pressure on the plane.

▶ **2** Alternatively, plane a small bevel at the end of the wood, so that the fibers slope away and are not touched by the plane blade, but remain to give support.

Repairing splits and tears

■ If the end grain splits while planing, simply ease some glue into the split with a slip of paper and then clamp it or wrap it with masking tape. When the glue has dried, replane using a supporting block.

■ If a section of wood lifts and tears when planing an edge, remove the tearout by making two angled saw cuts with a fine-bladed saw; make sure that the two cuts meet without crossing. Cut a plug from matching stock, then glue and clamp it in position. When dry, replane carefully.

End grain split

Edge split

Planing end grain

◀ **1** End grain will split if the fibers are not supported at the end of the stroke. If the board is wide enough, plane the end grain first from one direction, then from the other. Take care to lift the plane at the end of each halfway stroke. This technique pushes the fibers together, compressing them rather than splitting them.

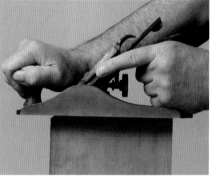

▼ **3** Another method is to fit a supporting block of scrapwood at the end of the main piece, making sure that they are level. If the block is too high, it will obstruct the plane blade; if it is too low, it will not support the fibers of the main piece and they will still split. It is easier to use a block plane to plane the end grain of small pieces. Hold it in one hand, with your palm over the lever cap and your fingers and thumb on either side. Exert pressure on the front of the plane with a finger, or the thumb of your other hand.

Using a shooting board

▶ 1 Similar to a bench hook, a shooting board is used to hold the wood and guide the tool when planing the edges and ends. Shooting boards that have a straight stop are designed for planing the wood square.

Straight stop

Angled stop

▼ 2 A miter shooting board has an angled stop for planing miters.

Using a spokeshave

▶ 1 Use a spokeshave to plane curves. Grip the handles on each side, and push the tool forward in short strokes in the direction of the grain. Rock it back and forth until you achieve a clean shaving, adjusting the blade setting if necessary. Use a flat-soled spokeshave for concave shapes, rotating the wood in the vise so that you are always cutting more or less horizontally.

◀ 2 Use a round-soled spokeshave for convex shapes, repositioning the wood as necessary in order to shave in the direction of the grain.

Power planing

A portable power planer is a useful tool for quick stock removal and for finishing wood. It has the advantage of being able to deal with long and heavy boards that would be cumbersome to plane by hand or feed through a jointer planer machine. The action of the planer can be quite vigorous, so hold it firmly and keep your hands well clear of the base. Adjust the depth of cut as required. The planer can be turned over and fixed in a special table to use as a mini-jointer planer. With its fence attached, you can square wood quite easily.

Machine planing

A jointer planer can prepare the face side and face edge of the wood in the jointer on top of the machine; in this mode it is hand-fed. It can also make the opposite side and edge parallel and flat in the thickness planer underneath; it is equipped with automatic feed for this operation. The longer the table, the flatter and straighter the results. Take care to keep your fingers well away from the cutter block; always use the cutter-block guard, and only use the machine for pieces 12 in. (300mm) or longer.

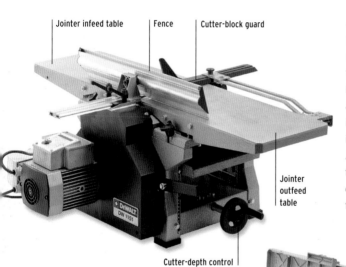

Jointer infeed table   Fence   Cutter-block guard

Jointer outfeed table

Cutter-depth control

Jointer depth of cut

Depth of cut is adjusted by raising or lowering the infeed table. The outfeed table should be level with the top of the cutters; adjust the infeed table so that it is slightly lower. This difference in height equals the depth of cut. As with hand planing, it is better to do several passes with smaller cuts. End with the finest cut for a smooth finish.

Thickness planer depth of cut

Depending on the machine, either both jointer infeed and outfeed tables, or just the latter, should be lifted to use the thickness planer below. The depth of cut is determined by the height of the thickness planer table in relation to the cutter block. Make several passes through the machine, with each cut no more than about 1/16 in. (2mm).

Thickness planer table

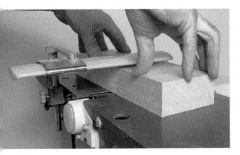

◀ Surface planing

Set the depth of cut and adjust the cutter-block guard so that the wood can pass underneath it. Pass the wood over the cutter from the infeed table, holding the wood at both ends with firm downward pressure. Walk the fingers across the guard to maintain the momentum. Use a pushstick to feed smaller boards across the machine.

Edge planing

▶ **1** Position the fence, checking that it is square to the jointer table. Position the guard so that it covers the cutter block up to the board. Feed the wood over the cutter, with the previously planed side pushed against the fence.

▼ **2** To plane an angled edge, set the fence to the desired angle and operate as before.

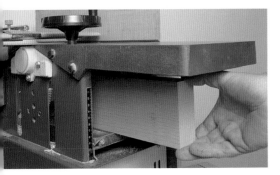

▲ Thickness planing

Set the depth of cut on the thickness planer and feed the wood across the table. The automatic feed rollers will engage with the wood and plane the piece; lift the wood from the planer at the other end of the table. Make a series of cuts to the desired dimension. Use the same technique to thickness both the surface and edge of the wood.

▼ End grain planing

Clamp the wood to a larger piece of scrapwood to make it easier to feed it across the cutters, then plane in the same way as edge grain. The cutter-block guard must be used in the normal way; it has been removed here for clarity only.

Squaring wood

When wood has been bought rough-sawn, or even ready-planed, it requires squaring to make sure that all surfaces are flat, adjacent surfaces are at 90 degrees to each other and opposite surfaces are parallel. The process of squaring wood is achieved by planing each surface in the following sequence: face side, face edge, width, thickness, ends. You can plane the wood square by hand, power tool or machine.

Face side

▶ **1** Select the best (face) side and plane it flat and smooth. To check the wood for flatness, place a straightedge across it. If the straightedge rocks or you can see light under parts of it, the piece is not flat. Move the straightedge around at different angles.

◀ **2** Use two steel rules or wooden strips (called winding sticks) to check for winding or twisting. Place one at each end of the board and sight across the tops; if they are parallel, the board is even.

Face edge

▶ **3** Select the best (face) edge and plane it flat and smooth. Use a try square to check that the face edge is at 90 degrees to the face side along its whole length. Be sure to push the stock of the square tight up against the face side of the wood. Hold the wood up to the light if possible. Once the face side and edge are perfectly straight and square, mark them with the face side and edge marks.

Eliminating ripples

If using a jointer planer machine, it is worthwhile running a piece of wood back through the machine after it has been planed on both sides completely on automatic feed to eliminate any small ripples.

Width and thickness

▲ **4** Use a marking gauge to mark the required width from the face edge; do this on both the face side and unplaned side of the board. Plane, or saw and then plane, the board to this width, checking frequently. Repeat this procedure to mark the required thickness from the face side. Again, do this on both the face edge and the unplaned edge of the board. Plane the board down to these marks.

▶ **5** Stop and check the work frequently, both for size and squareness.

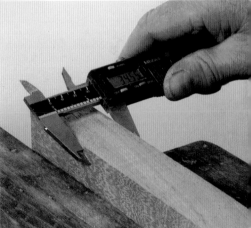

Ends

◀ **6** Square to length using a square, steel rule and marking knife. First, set the zero of the steel rule against one end of the wood and measure in about ¼ in. (6mm); this is the minimum amount of wood that can easily be cut off with a backsaw. Now move the steel rule so that the zero lines up with the ¼-in. (6mm) mark and measure the required length, leaving at least ¼ in. (6mm) at the other end. Use a square to mark all around the wood. Saw the board to length, then plane the end grain if necessary.

Chiseling

Of all hand tools, chisels are the most widely used. The chisel is used for cutting, trimming and shaping, and in particular for removing stock or waste in joint cutting. The chisel blade is beveled or sloped to a razor-sharp edge that has to be kept honed. In addition to keeping the chisel sharp, it is important that the cutting angle of the blade be maintained correctly. The action of chiseling is called paring, which is done vertically or horizontally, depending on the task. Sometimes, you will be working to cut away a complete end or face; at other times, particularly to make joints or to cut mortises, you only need to chisel partway through the wood.

SEE ALSO
Holding and clamping,
pages 24–25

Tool maintenance,
pages 92–99

Chiseling tools

The blade of a chisel is flat on the underside, with a beveled edge on the other. The end is sharpened. Chisels are pushed through the wood with the force of your hand; strong ones can be tapped with a mallet. All types of chisel come in a variety of widths; more cutting control is achieved with a narrow chisel, because it has less resistance from the wood, but a wider one produces a flatter and more accurate cut.

▶ Mallet

A carpenter's mallet is used to help drive chisels into wood when cutting mortises. It is usually made of beech, a very tough wood, and the striking action is slightly springier than with a hammer. Never use a hammer to hit a chisel. Mallets are also used for tapping joints together.

▼ Bevel-edged chisel

Bevel-edged (bench) chisels are lightweight, versatile tools. The sides of the blade are beveled as well as the tip, in order to give clearance for working in corners and joints, or where there are undercuts. They are used for trimming and shaping. They should not be used with a mallet.

▶ Firmer chisel

Firmer chisels have blades that are rectangular in section, making them more robust than bevel-edged chisels and suitable for general work rather than joinery.

◀ Mortise chisel

Mortise chisels are strong and heavy to withstand being hit with a mallet and to be used as a lever. They are used for cutting out deep recesses or mortises. Many mortise chisels have a steel band and shock-absorbing leather washer between the handle and blade.

Chiseling techniques

Always work to a marked line and work within the waste area, carefully paring away wood up to the line; remove only small amounts of wood at a time. The bevel of the blade should face toward the waste area. As a general rule, cut the wood across the grain first, then make any cuts along the grain afterward, to avoid splitting the wood.

◄ Paring vertically

Hold the handle in one hand and apply downward pressure from the shoulders to make a cut. Rest your other hand on the work and use it to guide the blade. Keep your elbows tucked in for greater accuracy.

▲ Paring horizontally

Hold the handle in one hand, with the forefinger extended along the blade for greater control. Use this hand to apply pressure; keep the forearm in line with the chisel, and elbow tucked in. Use your other hand to guide the blade. For additional power, lean into the work, applying body pressure from the waist.

Chiseling jigs

▶ **1** It is easy to make jigs to help you make more accurate chisel cuts. To trim the shoulder line of a tenon, for example, clamp a square-edged block of scrapwood so that it is perfectly aligned with the marked shoulder line, then press the chisel firmly against the vertical wall of the block to make the cuts.

▶ **2** Use an angled block of scrapwood to help you maintain a consistent and accurate angled cut.

Using a mallet

▶ **1** Normally, a chisel should be sharp enough to do its work without being hit by a mallet. Generally, you only hit a mortise chisel, or a firmer chisel, when removing waste from mortises.

◀ **2** When working across the grain, sever the fibers with a series of parallel cuts to loosen them before making the final cut to the line.

Powered chiseling (mortising)

◀ **1** If your work develops so that you have lots of mortises to make, a hollow chisel mortiser is a useful investment. This machine combines the pressing action of a sharp-edged chisel with a drill bit, which rotates within the hollow chisel to cut a square slot in a piece of wood.

▶ **2** Mortises of any width can be achieved by moving the piece along for each cut.

⚠ Safety tips

■ As with most cutting tools, do not make the mistake of substituting force for a sharp edge; this simply increases the chances of slipping and cutting yourself.

■ Use a vise, stop or clamp to hold the work steady; this will minimize the chances of hurting yourself.

■ Hold the chisel with both hands behind the cutting edge at all times. Use one hand to hold and guide the blade; use the other hand to hold the handle and supply the force required.

■ The long edges of new chisels can be sharp, so use a sharpening stone to blunt them.

Routing

The electric plunge router is probably the most creative tool in the workshop. It has become popular with woodworkers because it can do so many jobs that were once the province of specialized hand tools. Its simplest function is in converting a hole into a groove or dado by plunging the bit into and then across the wood. When you extend the range of bits and jigging devices, the router can also profile edges, cut through wood to any shape, cut joints, trim wood flat and much more. Despite its simplicity of concept, the router is indeed a very sophisticated shaping tool.

SEE ALSO

Holding and clamping,
pages 24–25

Measuring and marking,
pages 32–41

Tool maintenance,
pages 92–99

Plunge router

The plunge router is basically an electric motor with a sharp-edged rotating bit at the end of a spindle that is plunged into the wood to cut grooves, joints and a variety of shapes. Numerous bits and jigging devices are available for the router, making it an extremely versatile tool.

▲ Router bits

Router bits are either high-speed steel (HSS) or tungsten-carbide tipped (TCT). The latter are more expensive, but last many times longer. Bits come in a variety of shank diameters and a huge range of profiles. Generally, you use straight bits for cutting joints, and profile bits for shaping moldings. Some bits are self-guiding, which means that they can follow an edge or template accurately without any other guide.

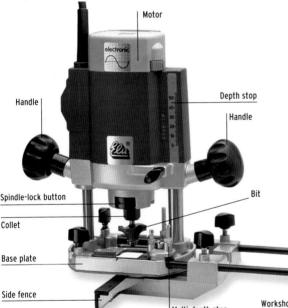

Motor

Depth stop

Handle

Handle

Spindle-lock button

Bit

Collet

Base plate

Side fence

Multi-depth stop

Workshop-made router templates

▶ Jigging devices and templates

The most basic jigging device is the adjustable side fence that is attached to the router. It is used for cutting straight grooves, dadoes and rabbets parallel to the edge of the wood. The fence can also be used for cutting mortise-and-tenons. Other jigs include a roller guide that allows parallel cuts to be made on a concave or convex edge, and a variety of guide bushes that allow the router bit to follow shaped templates. There are also jigs for cutting joints, such as a dovetail jig.

Routing techniques

The router motor is suspended on two steel columns and operates with a spring mechanism. When you press down on the handles, the cutting bit is plunged into the wood; when you release pressure from the handles, the spring mechanism raises the bit automatically. Adjust the depth stop to determine how deeply the bit cuts into the wood. Use the handles to guide the router along the required path.

▶ Inserting router bits

Make sure that the router is unplugged from the electricity supply, then turn it upside down and immobilize the spindle by pressing the spindle-lock button. Use a wrench to loosen the collet nut (the collet is the tapered sleeve that holds the bit on the end of the spindle). Insert the bit and tighten the nut. Some older routers do not have a spindle-lock mechanism, so a second wrench is needed to lock the spindle.

◀ Setting depth of cut

As a general rule, the depth of cut should be no more than half the diameter of the bit with any one cut; it is better to make a series of shallow cuts in order to achieve greater depth of cuts. Some routers have a single depth stop, while others have a multi-depth stop so that you can set a range of cuts for the job. A multi-depth stop (or turret stop) is simply a rotating cluster of screws and nuts, usually three. You set the height of the screws for three different depths of cut, and rotate the turret stop between passes to follow the sequence of cut depths.

Multi-depth stop

Basic plunge technique

▶ **1** With the bit locked in a raised position, place the router where required and switch it on. Release the plunge lock to plunge the bit into the wood as far as the depth stop. Immediately start to move the router steadily along the cutting line. Moving too fast may overload the motor; too slow may burn the work and damage the bit. With experience, the sound of the motor is your best guide.

▼ **2** At the end of the cut, release the plunge lock and let the bit retract from the work; it will spring up automatically. Switch off.

◀ Using a template

The use of a template and guide bush makes it easy to duplicate pieces of any shape. Roughly cut the workpiece oversize and secure the template to it with double-sided tape. Run the guide bush along the edge of the template, taking a series of cuts, if necessary, to shape the edge of the work.

Guide bushes and templates

Guide bushes are metal or plastic tubes or sleeves that attach to the router base and encircle the bit. When the guide bush is pressed against a template, it will guide the router so that the bit is always the same distance from the template. When attached, there will be a small gap (A) between the bit and the guide, and you need to allow for this gap when making the template. Calculate the size of the gap by deducting the radius of the bit from the radius of the guide. If A = ⅛ in. (3mm), for example, you would need to make the template ⅛ in. (3mm) smaller all around than the desired workpiece. Make the template from MDF or plywood.

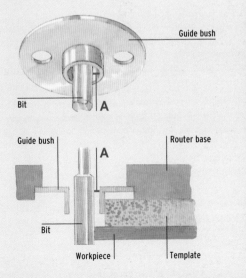

Guide bush

Bit **A**

Guide bush   **A**   Router base

Bit

Workpiece   Template

Grooves and dadoes

▶ **1** To cut a groove (or dado) parallel to the edge of the wood, mark the position of the groove on the wood and adjust the side fence so that the bit is aligned with the marked line. Guide the router along the line, keeping the side fence pressed against the wood. Make a series of passes for a deeper cut.

◀ **2** Use a batten instead of the side fence when the groove is not parallel to an edge, or on a wide board. Mark the groove position on the board, then calculate the distance (A) for the batten by deducting the radius of the bit from the radius of the router base.

▼ **3** Clamp the batten this distance from the marked line. Run the router against the batten to cut the groove.

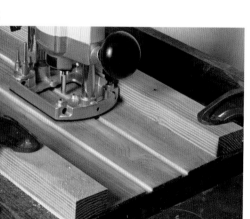

◀ **4** Use two battens when cutting a wide groove in the middle of a board. Position each one so that it allows the router to cut the sides of the groove, then rout out the center.

▶ **5** To rout a curved groove, remove the side fence and attach a trammel instead. Use double-sided tape to attach a piece of scrapwood to the workpiece where the center of the circle will be; locate the pin of the trammel in the scrapwood to protect the workpiece.

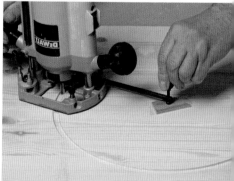

▶ Cutting a rabbet

Mark the dimensions of the rabbet on the wood. Set the side fence against the edge of the wood and use a straight bit to rout out the rabbet. Start at the edge and move inward to the marked line. Make a series of passes to reach the required depth.

◀ Shaped profile bits

Traditional moldings used to be cut with differently profiled hand planes, but the router has now largely replaced them. Self-guiding bits have a guide pin or ballbearing guide that runs along the edge of the wood below the rotating bit, so they can be used without a fence. If using non-self-guiding bits, use the same technique as for cutting a rabbet.

Direction of cut

Router bits rotate in a clockwise direction, so the machine tends to pull to the left as it is moved forward. It is therefore best to work counterclockwise around the outside edges of a workpiece, or clockwise around the inside edges. This will help to pull the bit tight against the edge.

Router table

▶ 1 Most routers can be turned upside down and attached to a special table, converting the tool into a mini-spindle molder. The position and height of the bit are adjusted, and the wood is passed across the table against the appropriate jig. In this case, a straight fence and straight bit are being used to cut a rabbet. Press the wood firmly into the base/fence as it passes over the bit, keeping fingers well clear.

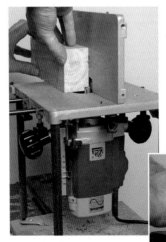

▼ 2 Here, the router table is set up with a wheel guide for profiling curved work; a radiused edge is being cut.

Drilling and hammering

The technique of drilling accurately is usually one of the first things learned in the workshop. A drill is essential, whether to drill holes for screws or to make the starter hole for a coping saw or jigsaw. Holes are drilled by the removal of wood fibers with a bit that is rotated at speed in the chuck of a hand or power drill. The fibers are severed and cleared from the hole by the drill flutings or grooves. Larger holes can also be cut by the scraping action of a spade (or flat) bit that is specifically designed for a power drill. Hammers are used to drive joints together and to nail them, as well as in the construction of mock-ups and workshop jigs.

SEE ALSO
Holding and clamping,
pages 24–25

Measuring and marking,
pages 32–41

Tool maintenance,
pages 92–99

Drills

Although hand drills are still used, they have for the most part been superseded by the more efficient power drill, which can be handheld or fixed in a stand.

Cordless drill

Twist bits

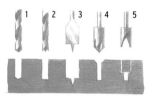

▲ Drill bit profiles

1 Twist bit for making small holes.

2 Doweling bit for setting wooden dowels that require a square-bottomed hole.

3 Spade bit for cutting large holes rapidly.

4 Countersink bit for allowing the screw head to lie level with the work's surface.

5 Plug cutter for removing waste in one piece so that it can be replaced later.

▶ Drill and bits

It is preferable to have at least a couple of different-sized drills, one small cordless battery-powered tool for fine work and a larger electric-powered one. Twist drill bits, which can have center points, are used for general work. Spade bits make it possible to cut larger holes, but using a narrow shank. All bits are available in a range of sizes.

Spade bits

◀ Drill stand

A portable drill stand permits more accurate drilling.

▶ Drill press

Also known as a pillar drill, this is the big brother of the power hand drill. A drill press that can take a mortising attachment is preferable. The drill press generally has a wide range of speeds, and is either floor- or bench-mounted with an adjustable table that can be raised or lowered. Floor-mounted machines allow you to drill long items.

Drilling

Variable-speed drills offer the most versatility. Start a hole at low speed, then increase the speed to suit the material once you have everything aligned.

Using a power drill

▶ **1** Insert the drill bit into the chuck and tighten it. Clamp the wood securely and mark the position of the drill hole with a cross. For end grain drilling, it is preferable to use a drill bit that has a clearly defined center point. You can also make a starter hole by twisting an awl into the wood.

▲ **2** Clasp your hands around the drill comfortably, positioning yourself above the work, and begin drilling. You can attach a depth stop to the drill bit, or simply wrap a piece of adhesive tape around it, to make sure that you do not drill in too far.

Depth stop

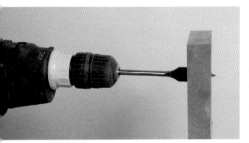

◀ **3** When drilling straight-through holes, stop drilling when the point of the bit appears through the wood, then turn the work around and drill from the other side; this is to prevent breakout (splitting).

▶ Using a drill stand

Using a drill stand allows more accurate drilling. Install the drill in the stand, making sure that it is secure, and insert the bit. Place scrapwood underneath the work for straight-through holes. For blind holes (holes that do not go all the way through), you will need to set the depth stop on the drill stand. Carefully hold down the work with one hand, anticipating the rotary snatching of the drill bit, then switch on the power with your other hand and gently lower the bit into the wood.

Hammers and fasteners

Different types of hammer are available to suit light or heavy tasks. They are categorized by weight rather than size. Nails and screws are used to reinforce joints (though they are seldom necessary for glued joints), serve as aids for alignment and act as holding devices to secure components. Screws are also used for attaching fittings, such as hinges.

◀ Claw hammer

A 16-oz. (450g) claw hammer is a good general-purpose hammer. The claw is used to extract bent nails. If you use a hammer to assemble joints, protect the wood from bruising with a piece of scrapwood.

▲ Nail set

Use a nail set to drive nails or brads slightly below the surface of the wood, without risking marking the wood with a hammer. You can putty over the hole. Use a set with a point that is slightly smaller in diameter than the nail or brad.

▶ Mallet

The head of a mallet is made from softer material than a steel hammer, so it can be used to hammer joints together without damaging the wood.

◀ Pin hammer

Use this lightweight cross-pein hammer for tapping in brads or veneer pins. Hold the pin and use the wedge of the hammer to start tapping it in, then finish driving in the nail with the striking face.

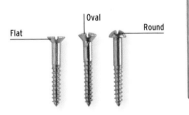

Flat   Oval   Round

▲ Fasteners

Cabinetmakers mostly rely on small wire nails, called brads, and narrow-diameter finishing nails to reinforce simple butt joints or miters and hold pieces while glue is drying. The common wood screw is mild steel or brass, and has a flat (countersunk), oval (raised) or round head. Hardened steel screws are used for finishing work.

▲ Screwdrivers

These are available in a variety of styles and sizes. It is important always to use exactly the right tip width for each task. Screwdrivers with an oval or bulbous handle are generally easiest to use.

Abrading

Before finishing a project, the whole surface must be flat and smooth.
It is sometimes possible for an expert to produce such a surface with
a plane, but normally you need to use abrading tools and techniques,
particularly on woods that have interlocking grain or other surface
difficulties. Abrading techniques are also used for fine shaping.
Abrading with a scraper produces an extremely fine silk-like shaving,
similar to that produced by chiseling. Sanding removes dust particles;
the sandpaper is applied in various grits, from coarse to fine,
to produce a progressively smoother finish.

SEE ALSO
Holding and clamping,
pages 24–25

Tool maintenance,
pages 92–99

Scrapers

Scrapers can produce a superior finish that does not require additional sanding. A cabinet scraper is generally used, although any sharp-edged sheet material will serve as a scraper, even a piece of glass. The long edges need to be sharpened to produce a burr of metal along the cutting edge before use. Scrapers can be used on any grain pattern because they cut so finely.

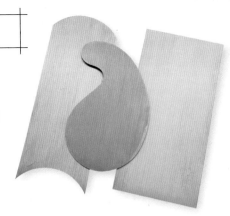

▲ **Cabinet scrapers**

Cabinet scrapers, made of quality steel, are used particularly for finishing veneered work and, because of their ability to remove very fine slivers, for removing excess glue. They come in different shapes for use on flat or curved surfaces.

Using a scraper

▼ ▶ **1** Hold the scraper in both hands, with the thumbs behind the blade. Use the thumbs to flex the blade as you push the scraper away from you. Start with the scraper vertical, then tilt it away from you until the burred edge is in contact with the wood. If you start producing dust and not shavings, then the scraper needs resharpening. Try to work with the grain or diagonally.

▶ **2** Scrapers become hot during use, and your thumbs can get sore, so you may find it more comfortable to hold the blade in a scraper holder.

▼ **3** Use the central screw to adjust the curvature of the blade.

Sanding materials

Sandpapers are graded by the coarseness of the grit (abrasive particles). Generally, you work through the grades from coarse to fine, until the wood is smooth and there are no visible sanding marks. A typical sanding sequence before applying a finish would be 100-, 180- and 240-grit sandpaper. Change the sandpaper when it begins to lose its bite and clog up with waste, and wipe the wood with a tack cloth between sandings to remove the dust.

1 Flint paper: This is used on raw softwoods and paintwork; it is not used for fine woodwork.

2 Garnet paper: This cuts cleanly, leaving a smooth surface, and is ideal for fine woodwork. It is available in very fine grit for hand, power or machine sanding.

3 Aluminum oxide paper: This tends to be harder than garnet paper and is often used with power or machine tools. It lasts longer, but does not give as fine a finish.

4 Silicon carbide paper: This is used by metalworkers as wet-and-dry paper, but furniture-makers use a self-lubricating type, used dry, that is ideal for rubbing a polished finish. Its hard grit can be used on manmade boards, which can be difficult to sand because of their high glue content.

5 Flexible paper: Flexible sandpaper, with aluminum oxide or silicon carbide grit, is designed for sanding curves and shaped areas.

6 Steel wool: In its fine grades, this is used for smoothing between coats of finish or for applying wax.

Grade	Grit	Application
Very coarse	40 60	Heavy shaping
Coarse	80 100	Shaping
Medium	120 150 180	Shaping and finishing
Fine	220 240 280	Finishing
Very fine	320 360 400 500 600	Final finishing, taking off sharp edges, sanding between coats of finish

6

Special sanding string is available for sanding intricate internal shapes.

1

5

4

2

3

Hand sanding

Always use a sanding block when sanding flat work by hand. However hard you try, if you simply hold the sandpaper in your hand, you will cause your smoothly planed or scraped surface to develop irregularities. A cork sanding block is firm, but slightly resilient. It should be a convenient size to fit your hand. Secure the work in a vise or clamp, and always wear a dust mask or respirator.

Cork sanding block

Using a sanding block

▶ **1** Tear a piece of sandpaper to fit around a sanding block; tear the paper against an edge, such as a steel rule, to avoid wastage. Hold the paper tightly around the block, with the bevels on top. Rub the paper along the grain with firm pressure. Never work across the grain, because this will create minute scratches that will be difficult to remove, and that may show when you apply the finish.

▼ **2** Generally speaking, wooden objects should not be left with sharp edges, so finish by softening all edges with fine sandpaper.

◀ ▼ Alternate forms

You can easily make different forms for sanding curves. For example, use a short length of plastic pipe as a form for concave sanding; place your fingers at each end to help stabilize the action. Wrap sandpaper around a stick to shape circular sections; hold the stick in one hand to sand, and rotate the work with the other. Alternatively, work a thin strip of sandpaper bath-towel fashion to form circular sections accurately.

Power and machine sanding

Sanding with a power or machine tool is generally quicker and more efficient than hand abrading methods. These tools provide the potential for fast stock removal and a fine finish. Sanders come in a variety of shapes and sizes, and as both handheld and static tools. An important feature of any sander is some form of suction device to remove the dust into a bag; you should also wear a dust mask or respirator.

▼ Disk and belt sander

Generally, this bench-mounted combination sander is most useful for smallscale pieces, but be very careful because it can easily remove too much wood. You need a precise approach for good results. You can use the fence and table on the disk sander as guides for sanding angles and end grain accurately.

▲ Portable belt sander

A belt sander has a continuous belt of sandpaper passing over a flat bed via two rollers. Designed for heavy-duty abrading and quick stock removal, it is also hard to control— it can ruin fine work by taking off too much wood.

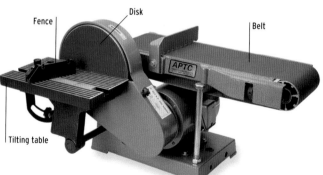

Fence

Disk

Belt

Tilting table

◄ Orbital sander

Sheets of sandpaper are clamped to the padded base plate of this finishing sander, designed to leave a scratch-free surface ready for finishing. The plate moves in an orbit rather than in a straight back and forth motion. A random orbital sander moves eccentrically while it rotates to create a random abrading effect. Smaller palm versions are available.

Belt sanding

▶ **1** Lift up the sander while you switch on the power, then place it on the workpiece and immediately start moving it. Hold it firmly, and never stop moving the sander as long as the belt is running. If you do, you are liable to gouge the wood. The danger is especially great on corners and edges, which can quickly be obliterated. Lift the sander from the workpiece before switching it off.

▶ **2** A belt sander can be inverted for flat and curved sanding. Clamp it to the bench and hold the work firmly as you feed it onto the sander.

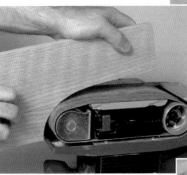

▼ **3** This narrow-belt sander can shape wood fast and furiously. Secure the work in a vise. The tool needs firm control directed at its tip, where it does the work.

◀ **Orbital sanding**
Let the weight of the tool do most of the work, and keep moving it up and down and across the work in gentle sweeping actions.

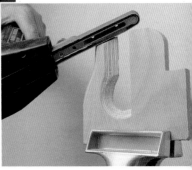

◀ **Disk sanding**
A disk sander is useful and accurate for sanding square, angled or curved end grain. Make sure that the work is fed into the rotation of the disk, so that the work is pushed downward and will not flip up. Tilt the table and angle the fence at the same time to shape a compound-angle cut.

Tool maintenance

All woodworking tools need maintaining, even if it is only a light coating of oil to prevent a steel blade from rusting. Many tools have a sharp cutting edge and, apart from those that are disposable when blunt, these edges need truing up, setting, honing and, in some cases, grinding to restore them to optimum working order. The importance of a razor-sharp edge for a marking knife, plane blade or chisel can only be emphasized by describing the effects of using blunt tools—a blunt marking knife tears rather than incises the grain, a blunt chisel fails to cut. Woodworking is about care, attention and pride, and this starts with your own tools.

Sharpening tools

To get the most out of your tools, you should maintain them regularly. Many new hand tools are supplied crudely sharpened, so the ritual of honing them to a razor-sharp edge should begin before their first use. Basic sharpening tools include a bench grinder, sharpening stones and a leather strop.

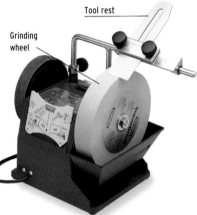

Tool rest

Grinding wheel

◀ Bench grinder

The bench grinder has coarse- and medium-grit wheels for repairing the edges of blades and touching up drill bits. Jigs, such as a tool rest, can be attached to help keep the angle of the grinding constant. Keep a jar of water nearby for cooling, because considerable heat is generated by grinding steel.

Synthetic oilstone

Waterstone

Natural oilstone

Slipstones

Diamond stone

▶ Sharpening stones

Bench stones for honing (sharpening) can be natural or synthetic oilstones, waterstones or diamond stones. Oilstones are hardwearing; waterstones cut faster but are more fragile; diamond stones are expensive but extremely durable and will cut carbide tools. All come in a range of grits, from coarse to fine; combination stones have a different grit on each side. Coarse grits can also be used for grinding. All sharpening stones require lubricant— oil for oilstones, water for waterstones and diamond stones. Slipstones are small shaped sharpening stones used for honing carving and turning tools.

◀ Leather strop

Most tools need to be polished on a leather strop after sharpening. A piece of soft leather can be stuck to a flat piece of wood, or folded around a length of dowel, depending on the tool being stropped. The strop should be treated with stropping paste.

Sharpening techniques

There are three stages to sharpening: grinding (rough sharpening), honing (fine sharpening) and stropping (polishing). Grinding is only needed when an edge is blunt or damaged, or after long use and much honing; always wear a face shield or safety glasses when grinding. Honing is the post-grinding procedure of rubbing the blade on a series of graded sharpening stones. Finally, the blade should be stropped on a piece of leather to polish the edge. The blade of a hand plane is sharpened in this demonstration, but the same basic techniques are used for other tools, such as chisels.

Grinding

◀ 1 Only grind a tool if the cutting edge of the blade is in any way damaged. With bevel downward, feed the blade against the wheel at the primary bevel angle (25 degrees for a plane blade); move the blade sideways across the wheel, using the fingers to maintain pressure at a fixed angle. Quench the tool often in water, to prevent the friction from bluing (heating) the edge of the blade and softening the steel (destroying the temper).

▼ 2 With bevel upward, lap the blade on a lapping board or sharpening stone. The blade must be pressed flat throughout the whole operation.

Lapping

■ Lapping is used to flatten the back of the blade and remove any scratches and burrs after grinding, and at intervals during honing.

■ Use a medium-grit sharpening stone or make a lapping board from a sheet of flat material, such as a board; cover it with fine-grit sandpaper, such as silicon carbide, garnet or aluminum oxide (see page 88). Use double-sided sticky tape to mount the paper.

■ Spread a few drops of oil onto the lapping board, then lay the blade flat on top of the board and rub it back and forth to achieve a smooth finish.

■ Check that you are lapping the blade thoroughly by coloring the back with permanent marker first, which should be removed by the lapping process.

Honing

◀ **1** Hold the blade, with bevel downward, on a coarse-grit sharpening stone to remove any deep scratches. Angle the tool so that the primary bevel is in contact with the stone, and make several dragging passes across the stone. Make sure that you lubricate the stone to avoid damaging the hardness of the steel.

◀ **2** The honing will have produced a burr on the tip of the blade. Lap the back of the blade on the stone to remove the burr. Repeat the honing and lapping process, progressing to a fine-grit stone to achieve a finer finish. For final honing, lift the blade slightly to achieve the correct angle for the secondary cutting bevel.

◀ **Stropping**

With bevel upward, drag the edge along a leather strop to remove the final burr.

Bevel angles

■ Chisels and plane blades have two bevel angles. The ground angle, in which condition the tool is normally bought, is about 25 degrees; the sharpened angle, which is put on during honing in the workshop, is 30–35 degrees.

■ Grinding or honing a chisel blade at a slightly shallower angle increases its cutting efficiency, but makes the tip more brittle.

■ A number of special jigs are available to help hold the tool at the required angle.

■ To ensure that the ground angle is maintained, color part of the bevel with permanent marker. Place it in position and rotate the grinding wheel by hand for half a revolution to remove some of the marker. This will tell you if the tool rest needs to be adjusted.

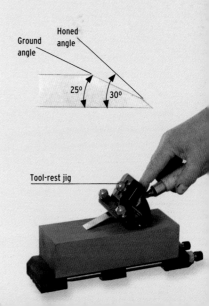

Ground angle / Honed angle / 25° / 30°

Tool-rest jig

Hand plane mechanics

After sharpening a plane blade, it is important that it is reset in the plane body correctly. It is a good idea to take a plane to pieces to familiarize yourself with its component parts.

■ The plane blade is basically a wide chisel held in a finely adjusted jig (the plane body). Various controls are used to adjust the amount of blade protruding through the mouth of the plane, and ensure that the blade is parallel across the mouth and therefore will not cut grooves in the wood at one corner of the blade or the other.

■ A cap iron is attached to the upper surface of the plane blade; its slightly hooked tip is positioned $1/8$ in. (2-3mm) from the blade tip. This gives reinforcement to the blade tip, and also causes the shaving to curl over and clear. Each time the blade is sharpened, the cap iron has to be removed, so its proper replacement is important.

■ The angle of the blade in the plane body is set at 45 degrees. The edge of the plane blade is normally ground to a primary bevel of about 25 degrees, and its tip is honed to a secondary bevel of about 30-35 degrees. Bench planes have the bevel of the blade facing down; block planes have the bevel facing up. Differences in the plane body result in both types of plane having an overall cutting angle of about 45 degrees.

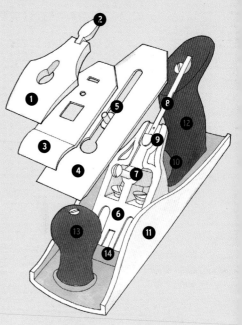

Anatomy of a plane

1 Lever cap	9 Depth adjustment lever
2 Locking lever	10 Depth adjustment knob
3 Cap iron	11 Sole
4 Blade	12 Rear handle
5 Cap iron locking screw	13 Front knob
6 Frog	14 Mouth
7 Lever cap screw	
8 Lateral adjustment lever	

◀ Sighting the plane

This is the process of checking that the blade is set correctly. Turn the plane upside down and look down the sole to determine how far the blade protrudes and whether the cutting edge is set parallel to the sole; use a sheet of white paper to help you to see this better. Use the depth adjustment knob and lateral adjustment lever to adjust the blade so that it protrudes fractionally, giving a parallel shadow. Set the plane to take a fine cut at first until you are used to the action. There is less resistance and more control than if you set the blade to take a thicker cut. As you plane, adjust the blade until you are taking a good shaving from the surface.

Sharpening a cabinet scraper

▶ 1 Cabinet scrapers are sharpened by turning a burr on both sides of their scraping edges. Using a sharpening stone, lap the scraper on both sides to remove any remaining burr.

▶ 2 Hone the edges on the stone, progressing to a fine finish on a fine-grit stone.

▶ 3 Use a burnisher (a hardened steel rod) to put a burr on the edges. Press or clamp the blade onto the bench, jutting over the edge slightly. Burnish the scraper edge, using as much pressure as you can. Start at the corner nearest you, with the burnisher handle downward, so that the rod leans over the blade slightly. Rub away from yourself and slightly downward. A few strokes should be sufficient for each edge.

◀ Cleaning an oilstone

Clean oilstones with mineral spirits. Flood the surface and let it soak, then wipe off. If the surface is sticky with blobs of resin, use a stiff brush to clean them off. Be sure to wear goggles and rubber gloves. After cleaning, and to flatten the surface, color the face of the stone with a permanent marker, and then rub the stone face on a lapping board until the color has worn away (see page 94). Some woodworkers recommend using a diamond stone to lap old oilstones.

Sharpening a saw

The saw is a difficult tool for an amateur to sharpen. Nowadays, most woodworkers send them to a "saw doctor" rather than try to do it themselves. In addition, many hand- and powered saws have hard-tipped blades that are not resharpenable; they offer many times the life of traditional blades, and are thrown away when dulled.

Power tool maintenance

Power and machine tools can be a great help in the workshop, but only when they are working well. Careful maintenance is important both for function and for safety. Here are some general guidelines, but always refer to the tool's manual and follow the manufacturer's recommendations.

Router and bit maintenance

◀ **1** The router creates a lot of dust, and it is the dust that can be a menace to its proper efficiency. You should routinely clean out all the dust and debris. Start by vacuuming it well, then use a small brush to get the dust out of all the little nooks and crannies. Polish the poles and generally keep all the metalwork gleaming.

◀ **2** After cleaning, spray a small amount of light oil on the various moving parts so that they can move freely, and wipe the whole works with a lint-free cloth. Note that routers need to be stripped down for a more thorough cleaning every now and again; refer to the manufacturer's instructions.

Check the bearings of self-guiding bits regularly for wear.

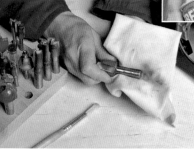

◀ **3** Router bits are expensive and brittle, and the gradual build-up of wood resin results in wear and bit slippage. Use a brush, cloth and mineral spirits to clean away the resin. Do not be tempted to polish the shank or collet with steel wool, because repeated cleanings will make for a loose fit. Apply a thin smear of light oil afterward.

▶ **4** Carefully hone the inside edges of bits on a sharpening stone; use a diamond stone for tungsten-carbide bits. Do not hone the outside edges, because this would disturb the precisely balanced cutting action.

Checking squareness on a table saw

◀ **1** A table saw must cut square, otherwise it is useless. You need to check squareness after changing blades and at regular intervals along the way. Set an engineer's square (the metalworker's equivalent of a try square) in the miter fence slot so that it slides smoothly. Take two measurements, one from the front edge of the blade, and one from the back. If the two are identical, then the blade is aligned with the miter slot. If they are not, you must realign the blade so that it is parallel to the miter slot.

▶ **2** Set the square vertically against the blade to check that the blade is at right angles to the table, and make adjustments accordingly.

▼ **3** Check the clearance between the blade and the throat plate; adjust as necessary to match the manufacturer's recommendations.

◀ **4** To prove squareness, use a try square to draw a line all the way around a piece of scrapwood. Butt the board up against the miter fence and feed it into the blade. Run a cut half the width of the board. Turn the board over and cut from the other edge. Stop when the two cuts are ¹⁄₈ in. (3mm) apart.

⚠ Lubrication

Lubrication needs to be near the top of your safety checklist. Machine surfaces occasionally need to be wiped over with light oil or wax, and moving machine parts need to be lubricated according to the manufacturer's instructions. If you hear squeaks and groans when you power up a machine, the chances are that it needs lubrication. If a moving part is badly in need of lubrication, it might fail catastrophically.

▶ **5** If the two cuts meet, then squareness is proved. If they are out of alignment, you need to run checks on the blade, the table and the miter fence.

The saw cuts should meet.

3
Jointing techniques

Step-by-step instructions on forming
a variety of basic woodworking joints

Principles of wood jointing

Most woodworking consists of joining pieces of wood together for a variety of purposes—for changing shape, creating structure, maximizing strength or dealing with wood movement. A well-designed joint is strong, visually attractive or cleverly hidden and, above all, survives the passage of time, when constant shrinking and swelling of the fibers affect its structure.

Joint strength

▼ **1** An end-grain-to-end-grain glue joint is the weakest, because there is no fiber overlap and the glue is absorbed down the grain, leaving too little on the matching surfaces. Subsequent wood movement can cause the joint to come apart over time.

◀ **2** End grain glued to any other grain has much reduced bond strength. An end-grain-to-long-grain glue joint will also shrink across the grain more than along the grain, which will stress the glue line.

▶ **3** The strongest glue joint occurs when two similar grain directions meet side by side, in effect continuing the figure of the wood. Any shrinkage that occurs will be consistent, because both pieces behave in the same way.

Wood movement

A simple rule is that wood tends to move across the grain rather than along it, and the growth rings (visible on the end grain) will try to straighten out. Try to use quartersawn wood (with short rings on the end grain); this will minimize wood movement.

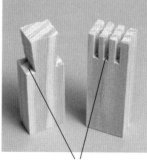

◀ **4** By introducing a shoulder to the joint, it becomes mechanically stronger, because there is maximum long-grain fiber overlap and maximum glue area. These joints also offer great visual interest.

Shoulders

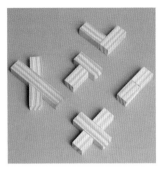

◀ **Joint configurations**

◀ Joint configurations

There are basically four jointing configurations: L, T, X and I. There are also angled variations of these types. Each configuration can be achieved by a variety of joints. For example, rabbet, lap, miter, dowel, dovetail and mortise-and-tenon joints can all be arranged in the L configuration.

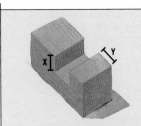

X–Y rule

A basic rule is to avoid short grain. When cutting a joint close to the end of a piece of wood, the depth of the cut (X) must not exceed the length of the piece remaining on the end (Y). If it does, this short grain will certainly break. This is because the pressure or leverage to which the joint is subjected is too great for the short grain over the reduced area.

▼ Sawn and milled elements

The elements of a joint fall into two categories: sawn and milled. Sawn elements can be completed by one cut, such as a miter; milled elements are part of a step-by-step process, such as a rabbet. No single tool or method is the only option for making these elements. As well as the methods described in this chapter, refer to Chapter 2 (pages 28–99) to explore other options.

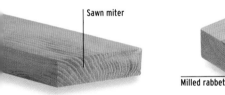

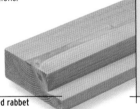

Sawn miter

Milled rabbet

Stresses on joints

Before the basic orientations of wood are jointed and put into service, it is worth analyzing the forces that the joints have to resist. An awareness of the mechanical stresses on joints will help you to predict potential problems and solve them with the right joint.

    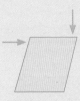

Tension
Force that pulls a joint apart.

Compression
Force that pushes a joint in on itself.

Shear
Push/pull stress on a glue line.

Bending
Tendency of wood to flex and pull a joint apart.

Racking
Joints bending in unison, causing changes of angle in a structure.

Choosing a joint

Many joints have evolved over the centuries to meet specific functional requirements, such as the mortise-and-tenon and dovetail joints in frame and carcass construction. As such, joints embody a rich and longstanding wood culture, most notably the dovetail. There are hundreds of joints in existence, and your choice of joint will usually be based on both its function and appearance.

▶ Fasteners and knockdown joints

There are occasions when temporary joinery is more convenient for large and restless pieces of furniture, or no joinery at all may be more suited to the purpose or status of the structure. Woodworking accommodates these contingencies with joints that disassemble and reassemble (knockdown joints), and with a range of screws, fasteners and reinforcements.

Butt joint with commercial cross-dowel connecting screw.

Jointing manmade boards

Manmade boards, such as particle board and MDF, are less prone to wood movement than solid wood. In addition, board materials have little localized mechanical strength, and break away at the edges if traditional joints are used. These materials exploit modern machine jointing methods, such as biscuit and dowel joints. Manmade boards can be miter jointed in order to conceal the core; otherwise, use an edge banding (see page 114).

Matching joint to structure

▲ **Panel**
Use a simple rubbed-glue edge joint, or strengthen by mechanical means with tongue and groove, loose splines, dowels or biscuits.

▼ **Flat frame**
Use mitered butt joints, lap joints, dowels or mortise-and-tenons. When using manmade board, try to cut frames from the whole board.

▲ **Rail-and-stile or underframe**
Use mortise-and-tenons, either through, stopped or wedged. Joining this arrangement in manmade board is not appropriate.

▼ **Partition**
Use a dado. You could also use a dado for manmade board, but a tongue, biscuit or dowel joint may be sufficient.

▲ **Corner**
Use a dovetail, or a simple butt, mitered butt or rabbet joint reinforced with dowels or biscuits.

Joint	Strength	Uses
Butt and rabbet (pages 110–111)	No real strength; rabbet is slightly stronger than a butt joint; can be reinforced with nails, screws, splines, tongue and groove, dowels or biscuits	Join individual boards into a longer unit for tabletops and long panels; simple carcassing; lightweight frames; small boxes where top and base add strength. Mitered butt joints are useful aesthetically because they continue the line of grain around the piece and conceal the core of manmade boards. Similarly, most of the end grain is hidden in a rabbet joint, so use it instead of a butt joint when a better appearance is required
Edge and scarf (pages 112–115)	Not very strong; can be reinforced with splines, tongue and groove, dowels or biscuits	Join individual boards into wider or longer units for tabletops and panels
Dowel (pages 116–117)	Strong; quick and easy alternative to a mortise-and-tenon; ideal for manmade boards	Cabinet frames; doors; tabletops; table frames; chair frames; boxes
Biscuit (pages 118–119)	Quick and strong, but not as strong as traditional joints; ideal for manmade boards	Tabletops; drawer sides and base; simple carcasses and frames (but not the corners of frames); small boxes
Lap (pages 120–121)	Not very strong	Small simple frames; cabinet door frames
Dado (pages 122–125)	Effective and easy	Attaching shelves and dividers inside cabinets; holding rails inside carcasses
Mortise-and-tenon (pages 126–131)	Very strong and rigid	Cabinet frames; table underframes; chair frames; door frames; leg assemblies; carcasses
Dovetail (pages 132–137)	Very strong and attractive	Boxes; drawers; cabinets; shelves

Gluing and clamping

Most items of woodwork rely on glue to hold the joints together. Modern woodworking glues are stronger than the surrounding wood fibers, and when something breaks, it is unlikely to be along the glue line. Make sure that all surfaces are clean and grease-free before gluing. Most joints need to be clamped to provide constant pressure while the glue cures (dries). Remember to protect the workpiece with blocks of scrapwood under the clamp heads. Always have a dry run without glue first, to check that you have everything you need and that everything is positioned correctly.

◀ Clamping a panel

Use bar clamps when gluing boards together to form a panel. You will need a clamp at each end, plus one or more across the center. Position the clamps alternately above and below the panel to prevent it from bowing under pressure. Lay the bottom clamps on the bench; glue the joints, tighten the clamps and wipe away any excess glue. Then locate and tighten the upper clamps.

Clamping a frame

▶ 1 Use a pair of bar clamps, making sure that the center of each clamp aligns with the center of the thickness of the wood. Use a try square to check that the frame is square, adjusting the clamps if necessary.

SEE ALSO
Holding and clamping,
pages 24–25
Types of glue,
pages 108–109

▶ 2 Check the diagonals of frames (and carcasses) by placing a rod diagonally from corner to corner. The opposing diagonals must be exactly the same.

▲ Clamping a carcass

The principles of clamping and checking squareness and diagonals are similar to those applied when clamping a frame. However, a carcass consists of four sides with a top and base, so a lot of clamping is required. It can be clamped in stages (for example, the body first) or achieved all at once, using masking tape for initial alignment of the pieces. Here, virtually all available space has been taken up by C clamps.

Clamping a miter

▼ **1** Stretch a piece of masking tape across the center of the miter joint, then add more strips above and below. Repeat on the other side of the wood to equalize the pressure.

▶ **2** Alternatively, use a hot-melt glue gun to attach two 45-degree blocks of scrapwood to the outside of the miter joint. Align a C clamp with the center of the glue line on the miter, so that the clamp applies pressure all along the joint. When the glue is dry, chisel or saw off the scrapwood blocks and plane the edges.

Clamping positions for best bond

All surfaces of the joint should be pulled in snugly, but the direction of clamp pressure is best applied where it enables long-grain contact for the strongest glue bond.

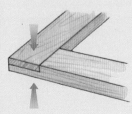

Pressure joins long grain of lap-joint cheeks.

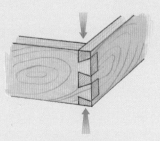

Glue bond is between interlocking dovetails and pins.

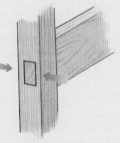

Clamp tenon face to mortise cheek.

Types of glue

	PVA (white glue)	Aliphatic resin (yellow glue)	Dry hide glue	Polyurethane	
Wood and wood materials	Yes	Yes	Yes	Yes	
Nonporous materials	No	No	Yes	Yes	
Preparation/mixing	No	No	Yes	No	
Cure method	Solvent evaporation	Solvent evaporation	Solvent evaporation	Moisture catalyzed	
Open time	Average	Average	High	Average	
Clamp time	Average	Average	None to average	Average	
Water-resistant	No	No	No	Yes	
Waterproof	No	No	No	Yes	
Sandable	No; gums up	Yes	Yes	Yes	
Gap-filling	No	No	Yes	No	
Reversible/repairable	Yes	No	Yes	No	
Thermoplastic (creeps)	Yes	Yes	No	No	
Bonds oily or resinous wood	Yes; with acetone wash	Yes; with acetone wash	Yes; with acetone wash	Yes	
Water or solvent clean-up	Water	Water	Water	Solvent	
Cost	Low	Low	Low	Moderate	
Safety	No	No	No	Potential skin sensitivity; fumes	

Resorcinol formaldehyde	Urea formaldehyde (plastic resin)	Epoxy resin	Cyanoacrylate (superglue)	Contact cement
Yes	Yes	Yes	Yes	Yes; not for structural bonds
No	No	Yes	Yes	Yes
Yes	Yes	Yes	No	No
Catalyzation	Catalyzation	Catalyzation	Moisture catalyzed	Solvent evaporation
High	High	High	None	High
High	High	High	Temporary immobilization	None
Yes	Yes	Yes	Yes	Yes
Yes	No	Yes	No	No
Yes; dust toxic	Yes; dust toxic	Yes; difficult	Yes	No
Yes	No	Yes	Yes	No
No	No	No	No	Yes
No	No	No	No	Yes
Yes; with acetone wash	No	Yes	Yes	No
Water	Water	Solvent	Solvent	Water for water-based type only; also solvent
High	Moderate	High	Very high	High
Formaldehyde gas fumes	Formaldehyde gas fumes	Toxic until dry; irritant	Bonds skin; eye irritant	Toxic fumes; flammable

Butt and rabbet joints

The butt joint is the simplest of joints. Butt joints have no integral strength, because the mating surfaces do not interlock; they simply butt against each other. For this reason, they are usually reinforced in some way—for example, with pins, screws, dowels, biscuits or splines. The rabbet joint combines a butt on one piece with a stepped cutout (rabbet) on the other. This gives slightly more mechanical integrity, and also creates a longer glue line for greater strength. A rabbet joint can also be reinforced.

◄ Butt joint

Although glue alone will hold the joint together, it is not a very strong or permanent bond, because the end grain absorbs much of the glue, and end-grain gluing should generally be avoided in woodworking. Subsequent wood movement can cause the joint to come apart over a period of time. Reinforcement with dowels or biscuits greatly strengthens this joint.

▶ Mitered butt joint

A miter joint consists of two pieces with their ends cut at 45 degrees that meet to form a right angle. A typical example is the corner of a picture frame, but the joint can also apply to the corner of a carcass. Miter joints are visually pleasing, because there is no visible end grain. However, it is still just an end-grain butt joint whose only strength comes from the type of glue holding it together. A very light frame glued with epoxy might survive a low-stress application, but most frame miters need reinforcement to last.

◄ Compound miter joint

Combining a miter angle with a tilt of the saw blade creates a compound miter. These miters tilt the sides of boxes and stave constructions outward or inward. The miter saw or table saw makes quick work of compound cutting, but like any miter, accuracy is critical. Again, this type of joint is weak and benefits from reinforcement.

Making a rabbet joint

▶ **1** Cut the boards to size and plane them square. Set a marking gauge to the thickness of the wood and mark a line on the inner face of the rabbet piece; extend this line onto the edges to about two-thirds the thickness of the wood. Reset the gauge to one-third the thickness of the wood. With the stock held against the face side, mark along the end grain, extending the line along the edges to meet up with the marked shoulder line. Shade in the waste area.

▶ **2** Holding the wood upright in a vise, use a tenon saw to cut along the line scribed across the end grain; saw down to the shoulder line. Use both hands on the saw for extra control.

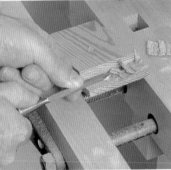

◀ **3** With the wood clamped face down or held against a bench hook, saw along the shoulder line and remove the waste. Clean up the rabbet with a chisel; use a try square to check that it is square. Glue and clamp together.

Power methods

It is much faster to cut rabbets with power tools. For example, clamp the piece to the bench and use a router with a straight bit and fence to rout out the stepped portion. You can clamp several pieces together to rout them all in one go.

▼ **Rabbet joint**

The rabbet joint is easy to make, but not very strong.

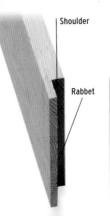

Shoulder

Rabbet

Edge and scarf joints

When wide boards are required, it is usually necessary to join together narrower pieces along their edges. The simplest way to do this is to butt-joint the boards edge to edge. For a stronger bond, the joint can be reinforced with a spline, tongue and groove, dowels or biscuits. When long boards are required, shorter pieces can be joined using a scarf joint, where two beveled ends are glued together.

SEE ALSO

Holding and clamping, *pages 24–25*

Measuring and marking, *pages 32–41*

Sawing, *pages 42–61*

Planing, *pages 62–71*

Chiseling, *pages 72–75*

Routing, *pages 76–81*

Gluing and clamping, *pages 106–107*

◀ **Butted edge joint**

A butted edge joint is strong enough for most purposes; it can be glued without clamps by rubbing the tacky glue surfaces together. However, rubbed joints cannot be sprung, because without clamping, edge contact will not occur. Rubbing is suitable for edge joints under 1 yd. (1m) long. The surfaces must be perfectly square and true for this joint to be successful.

▶ **Mitered edge joint**

A butted miter joint, called a waterfall joint because the grain pattern tumbles down over the joint, has grain orientation that is strong for gluing, but careful clamping is required to avoid slippage.

Grain pattern

■ Quartersawn wood remains relatively stable on drying; plainsawn wood tends to warp, as the growth rings on the end grain straighten out. When using plainsawn wood, it is best to alternate the rings into a herringbone configuration to help prevent bowing.

■ The grain on the surface of the boards can be matched to create different effects, such as slip or book matching.

Slip matches always keep the same face up.

Book matches alternate between top and bottom faces.

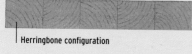

Herringbone configuration

Butted edge joint

▼ **1** Cut the boards to size and plane them square. Number them in the order in which they will be assembled. With face sides outward, place the first two boards together in a vise and plane the edges that are to be joined. Try to plane the edges square to the face sides; however, by planing them as a pair, they will still fit together even if they are not perfectly square.

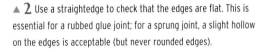

▲ **2** Use a straightedge to check that the edges are flat. This is essential for a rubbed glue joint; for a sprung joint, a slight hollow on the edges is acceptable (but never rounded edges).

◄ **3** Continue planing the pairs of edges that are to be joined on all the boards. Glue together, clamping if required. When dry, clean up the surface of the jointed board with a plane.

▲ Rubbed glue joint

A butt joint can often be glued without clamping if the edges are perfectly flat and square. Apply the glue, then place the both pieces flat on a workbench (protected with paper). Use a sliding motion to rub them together vigorously. This squeezes out the glue and creates a suction. Wipe off the excess glue with a damp cloth and allow the panel to dry.

▲ Sprung joint

Greater moisture loss at the end of the boards can cause shrinkage that pulls an edge joint apart. This can be overcome by using a sprung joint. The edges are planed so that they are slightly concave along their length—just a $1/32$-in. (1mm) concavity (exaggerated in the picture above for clarity). The boards are glued and clamped together; this creates greater tension at the ends of the boards. Later, any end-grain shrinkage will relieve this tension instead of creating it.

◀ ▶ Splined edge joint

Splining is a quick and easy way to reinforce an edge joint. If referenced from the marked face, it takes little calculation of layout for an accurate joint with perfect alignment of the faces. Splining also prevents slippage until the glue has dried. Manmade materials work well for splines; the spline needs to be twice the depth of the groove. By use of a contrasting material, the spline can form an attractive detail. The spline can run the entire length of the boards, or it can be stopped short so that it will not be exposed at the ends. Stopping the spline also means that any later shaping of the edge will not expose it.

Edge treatments

Edge bandings are generally applied to manmade board that is to be veneered; the bandings can be made of solid wood or veneer. They can be attached using any of the edge jointing methods—glue only, tongue and groove, spline or biscuit. After the panel has been veneered, the edges can be profiled as though they were solid wood, provided the edge banding is wide enough; ideally, it should be at least ¼ in. (6mm) wide. Edge profiles were traditionally cut with special hand planes, but the router has now largely replaced them.

◀ ▼ Tongue-and-groove edge joint

This joint is best known for its use in good-quality flooring. The tongue is like an integral spline that reinforces and aligns the joint, but takes a little more calculation to cut. Boards must be cut wider to provide material for the tongue. Cut a groove along one edge and a corresponding tongue along the other edge of each board. You can do this by hand, using a tenon saw and chisel, but it is quicker to use a machine saw or a router with special tongue-and-groove bits.

Glue only

Tongue and groove

Spline or biscuit

Scarf joints

The shallow angle of the basic glued scarf joint exposes long-grain surfaces for a good glue joint. A slope ratio of 1:8, with 1 being the thickness of the wood and 8 the length of the taper, is usual. Simple gluing bonds the parts into a unit that theory says is as strong as a single board. Like edge joints, there is no perfect solution to orienting the growth rings of solid wood scarfed parts—either to cup opposite to each other, or to cup in the same direction. Scarfs require careful clamping so that they do not slip while the glue dries.

▶ End-to-end scarf

Gluing boards end-to-end does not make a pretty joint, but it is very practical. This scarf can also be made into an angled piece, by aligning both parts bevel side up, and then gluing one bevel to the back of the other bevel to create an angle.

▲ Edge-to-edge scarf

You can reinforce the joint by adding a spline, in which case the extreme 1:8 angle can be reduced. If used to extend the length of structural woods, this joint should be reinforced with nails, screws or fixing plates.

▶ Worked scarf

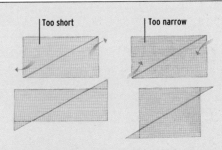

A worked scarf exposes more long grain for gluing, and also incorporates interlocking elements that award greater strength. Butted ends avoid the weakened, very thin material at the tail ends of conventional scarfs, but achieving a perfect fit demands great care and precision. The example shown here is just one of several ways of working scarf joints to improve their strength.

Adjusting board size

The scarf joint can be used to stretch out a too-short board by first ripping it diagonally, and then sliding the halves a little along the cutting angle, gluing and finally trimming to width when dry. The same principle can be used to make a too-narrow board wider.

Too short

Too narrow

Dowel joints

The dowel joint is a versatile and strong system of connecting wood, comprising two pieces butted together with a series of carefully aligned drill holes to accommodate wooden pegs, called dowels. You can buy special dowel jigs to drill dowel holes quickly and accurately, but you can also use homemade or proprietary dowel centers. Use at least two dowels in a joint; larger or heavier work may require more.

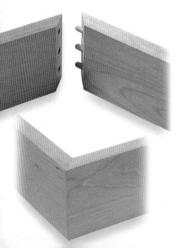

▲ ▶ Doweled butt joint

When used in place of a mortise-and-tenon, dowels should enter each mating part to a minimum depth of one-and-a-half times the dowel diameter. Used for alignment, dowels can be shorter.

◀ Doweled miter joint

Dowels are a good way of reinforcing a miter joint, but take care that the dowels are set inward enough from the face to ensure that they provide sufficient length for a good joint. Drill the holes in the end of one board and the inner face of the other, then cut the miter.

Dowels

- Dowels are usually made of a sturdy wood, such as beech or maple, manufactured in different diameters and lengths. Choose a dowel diameter one-third to half the wood thickness.

- A minimum of ³/₄ in. (19mm) of dowel should extend into each piece of the joint; the combined depth of holes should be slightly greater than the dowel length, to allow for a slight glue reservoir.

- Dowels have flutings or grooves to allow air to escape and the glue to disperse evenly. Without these, the dowel can act as a piston and compress the glue in the hole.

- Dowels are readily available to buy, but you can easily cut them yourself from a length of dowel rod. Use a marking gauge or saw to cut grooves in the dowel. Bevel both ends with a rasp, file or pencil sharpener.

◀ Proprietary dowel centers

Cut the boards to size and plane them square. Use a marking gauge and try square to mark the dowel positions on the first board. Drill the holes, then insert the dowel centers into them. Press these against the second board to mark the corresponding drill-hole positions.

SEE ALSO

Holding and clamping, pages 24–25

Measuring and marking, pages 32–41

Sawing, pages 42–61

Planing, pages 62–71

Drilling and hammering, pages 82–85

Gluing and clamping, pages 106–107

Improvised centers

▶ **1** Mark the positions for the dowels, then hammer a brad into each marked point. Cut the heads off the brads with pliers. Use the brads to mark the corresponding hole positions on the second board by pressing the pieces together.

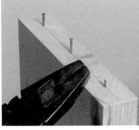

▶ **2** If making a T-shaped joint, use a try square to mark a guideline across the second board, with which you can align the edge of the first board. Separate the two boards, remove the brads with pliers and drill the holes.

▲ Drilling and assembly

Use a dowel bit with a center point to help you drill accurately on the marked positions. Attach a depth stop and take care to drill straight and square. Apply glue to the wood and the holes, but not the dowels because they may swell. Assemble the joint and clamp.

Dowel drilling jigs

◀ Workshop-made jig
To compensate for any deviation from 90 degrees, always drill mating parts from opposite sides of the jig.

◀ Proprietary jig
These have different hole sizes for different dowel diameters.

Biscuit joints

A biscuit joint is simply a butted joint strengthened by elliptical wooden inserts called biscuits. A biscuit jointer (also known as a plate jointer) is a small-diameter circular saw with a plunging cutter. It is used to cut elliptical slots into the wood; the biscuits are then glued into the slots. The glue causes the biscuits to swell and fill the space. Some biscuit jointers can also be used to cut grooves along the wood, such as a slot for a drawer bottom.

SEE ALSO

Holding and clamping, *pages 24–25*

Measuring and marking, *pages 32–41*

Sawing, *pages 42–61*

Planing, *pages 62–71*

Gluing and clamping, *pages 106–107*

Main handle

Secondary handle

Adjustable fence

Sole plate

Biscuits

Blade aperture

◀ ▲ T-configuration biscuit joint

Biscuits have a little side-to-side play in the kerf for joint adjustment during gluing, so marking does not have to be precise. When inserting a dry biscuit into a slot, the biscuit should be a snug fit across the thickness. Use water-based glue to ensure that the biscuit swells to create a strong joint.

Biscuit spacing

The spacing of the biscuits is not critical; every 2 or 3 in. (50 or 75mm) is adequate. In thick-sectioned frames, the biscuits can be double-inserted across the thickness of the stock, but the joint should be used for center rails and not as a replacement for a mortise-and-tenon on corners of frames.

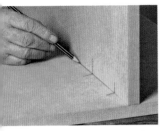

Cutting a biscuit joint

◄ **1** Cut the boards to size and plane them square. Mark pencil lines at the center points of the biscuit slots. For a T configuration, mark a squared line across the board to indicate the position of the adjoining board.

▶ **2** Clamp the board to the bench and set the cutter depth of the jointer. To cut slots along an end or edge, lay the tool on its side and align the cutter guide with the first mark; adjust the fence to center the blade on the wood. Plunge and then retract the cutter without disturbing the position. Repeat for each biscuit.

◄ **3** When cutting slots in the adjoining board for an L configuration, secure the board upright in a vise. Align the cutter guide and fence, and make plunge cuts as before.

▶ **4** For a T configuration, clamp a batten on the board to use as a guide for making plunge cuts.

▶ **5** For a miter joint, make the cuts so that the biscuit center will be slightly nearer the inner face of the board. Some jointers have a separate miter fence, or you could make one from an angled block of scrapwood.

▼ **6** Apply glue to the edges of the boards and in the slots. Insert the biscuits, assemble the joint and clamp.

Lap joints

Also known as a halving joint, the lap joint comprises two pieces, each reduced to half its thickness or width. The pieces are overlapped, so that the portion removed from one piece is replaced by the wood left on the other. The lap joint is very versatile, and can be arranged in various configurations. The basic technique for cutting all of them is the same, but the center lap joint is demonstrated here because it is the strongest and most commonly used.

Cheek

Shoulder

▲ End lap
An end lap has a single shoulder, and is formed by a deep rabbet cut to half the thickness of the wood. The joint can be reinforced with dowels, nails or screws.

Cheek

Shoulders

▲ ▶ Center lap
A double-shouldered center lap has a wide dado cut into the board anywhere along its length.

▶ T-lap
This is a combination of an end lap and a center lap. A stronger T-lap joint can be created by shaping the shoulders like a dovetail.

SEE ALSO
Holding and clamping, *pages 24–25*
Measuring and marking, *pages 32–41*
Sawing, *pages 42–61*
Planing, *pages 62–71*
Chiseling, *pages 72–75*
Routing, *pages 76–81*
Gluing and clamping, *pages 106–107*

Center lap joint

▶ **1** Cut the boards to size and plane them square. Position the two pieces together, and trace the width of the joint on the face of each piece. Using a try square, extend the marks across the face and halfway down the edges on each piece. These are the shoulder lines of the joint.

◀ **2** Set a marking gauge to half the thickness of the wood and score the depth lines between the shoulder marks. Shade the waste area.

▶ **3** Clamp the wood to the bench and use a tenon saw to cut halfway through the wood on the waste side of each shoulder line. Divide the waste wood with one or two more saw cuts.

◀ **4** Chisel away the waste wood between the shoulder lines. To avoid splitting the end fibers, work into the center of the recess from each side.

▶ **5** Check that the chiseled sections are flat and that the two pieces fit together, using a mallet or hammer (see page 85). Do any final trimming, then glue and clamp; when the glue is dry, clean up the surfaces with a plane.

Alternative methods

The halving cuts that form lap joints are basically dadoes (when in the center of the board) or rabbets (when at the end of the board). You can cut them quickly and easily using power or machine tools, such as a router or machine saw.

Dado joints

This simple joint comprises a crossgrain groove, called a dado, on one piece of wood into which another piece is fitted; it is also called a housing joint, because one part houses the other. A through dado consists of a groove that runs from edge to edge of the wood; a stopped dado has a groove that stops short of the front edge, so that the joint mechanism is hidden. There are several variations, such as the dovetail dado, in which the groove and matching tongue are dovetail-shaped.

SEE ALSO

Holding and clamping, *pages 24–25*

Measuring and marking, *pages 32–41*

Sawing, *pages 42–61*

Planing, *pages 62–71*

Chiseling, *pages 72–75*

Routing, *pages 76–81*

Gluing and clamping, *pages 106–107*

Shoulders

◄ Through dado

A through dado is not very strong; it has no mechanical resistance to tension, and there is no long-grain gluing contact. Use it for shelving and cabinet backs.

► Stopped dado

The dado groove can be stopped ³/₈–¹/₂ in. (10–12mm) in from the front edge; this is used to hide the joint mechanism on the front of shelving.

Stopped section   Notch

◄ Dovetail dado

The dovetail shape increases tension resistance. A dovetail dado is often used to join drawer sides and back. This example is a stopped dovetail dado.

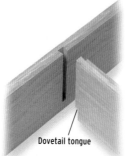

Dovetail tongue

Through dado

▶ **1** Cut the boards to size and plane them square. Use the housed element of the joint as a template to mark the position and width of the dado on the other piece.

Routing a through dado

After measuring and marking the dado, it is much easier and quicker to remove the waste using a router and straight bit. You can clamp several components together, with a guide batten across them, and rout several dadoes in one go. You can also cut dadoes using a machine saw.

◀ **2** Use a try square to extend the shoulder lines across the face of the wood. If necessary, extend the reach of the try square by placing a straightedge next to it. Continue the lines down the edges by one-third the thickness of the wood; this is the depth of the dado.

▶ **3** Set a marking gauge to one-third the thickness of the wood and mark the depth line on both edges. Shade the waste area.

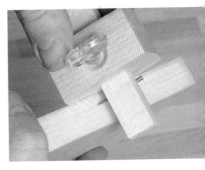

Handsawing jigs

■ Cut a batten whose height added to the dado depth equals the tenon saw blade measured from teeth to back. Clamp the batten across the wood at the marked line. The batten will act as a guide for both direction and depth of cut; when the back of the saw reaches the top of the batten, the dado is the correct depth.

■ Clamp a straight piece of scrapwood to the side of the saw, so that the base of the scrapwood is the dado depth above the saw teeth. This will act as a depth stop.

▼ **4** Clamp the wood to the bench and use a tenon saw to cut the shoulder lines. Make sure that you cut on the waste side of the lines. To make sawing easier on a wide panel, use a chisel to pare a shallow groove along the scribed lines, then use this groove to locate the saw.

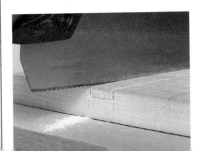

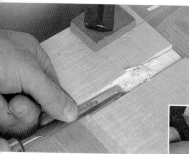

◀ **5** Chisel out the waste to halfway along the dado, working down to the bottom of the dado in a series of fine cuts. Turn the wood around and chisel in from the other side. If cutting a long dado, you will find a paring chisel useful; this is a bevel-edged chisel with an extra-long blade. Check that the base of the dado is flat, trimming as necessary.

▼ **7** Fit the two pieces of the joint together, using a mallet or hammer (see page 85). Make sure that the ends are level. Glue and clamp together.

▶ **6** Instead of a chisel, you could use a special hand plane, called a router plane, that has an adjustable hooked cutter. The base of the plane sits on each side of the dado, making it impossible to cut too deeply if the cutter is set to the correct depth.

Stopped dado

◀ **1** Use a marking gauge to scribe a line where the dado should stop, then finish marking the dado in the usual way. Chisel out the waste at the stopped end of the dado, paring vertically; remove the waste from the rest of the dado in the usual way, working inward from the open end.

▼ **2** The housed element needs to have a notch removed from the front corner to allow for the stopped dado. Use the marking gauge to scribe the dimensions of the notch, then cut it out with a saw. Finish the joint in the usual way.

Routing a stopped dado

If you use a router to cut a stopped dado, the stopped end will be rounded because of the curved shape of the bit. You can either round off the notch on the housed component using a chisel or sandpaper, or square off the stopped end of the dado using a chisel.

Dovetail dado

▶ **1** Using a router is by far the easiest way of making this joint. Mark the position of the dado, then use a straight bit to rout out the waste; clamp a batten to the wood as a guide. Rout the dado in stages, making several passes until you reach almost full depth.

◀ **2** Change to a dovetail bit. This cannot be lowered into the groove because of its shape, so it must be introduced into the wood from the side. Set the depth stop so that the bit achieves the full profiled cut in one pass. If making a stopped dado, you will need to withdraw the bit back along the dado. For a wider dovetail dado, place a thin strip next to the batten and use this as a guide for making a second cut alongside the first.

▶ **3** The best way to cut the dovetail tongue is to mount the router upside down in a router table and use the dovetail bit. Adjust the depth and width of cut, using the side fence as a guide. Pass the wood across the table to cut one side and then the other. If you do not have a router table, you can clamp the workpiece between two pieces of scrapwood, then use the router's side fence to rout along both sides of the piece to leave a dovetail-shaped tongue.

◀ **4** If you made a stopped dovetail dado, you will need to saw a notch off the end of the tongue. The end of the dado will be curved to match the shape of the bit, so round off the end of the tongue to match using a sharp chisel. Slide the two pieces together, then make any necessary adjustments. Glue and clamp in the usual way.

Mortise-and-tenon joints

Probably the most common woodworking joint, there are numerous variations of the mortise-and-tenon. The basic joint comprises a rectangular tenon (tongue) that fits snugly into a mortise (mouth). Generally, the tenon is cut on the horizontal pieces (rails), and the mortise on the verticals (stiles). The tenon and mortise should be about one-third the thickness of the wood. It is best to cut the mortise first, because it is the harder part to cut, and it is easier to adjust the tenon to fit it. A through mortise-and-tenon is demonstrated here.

SEE ALSO

Holding and clamping, *pages 24–25*

Measuring and marking, *pages 32–41*

Sawing, *pages 42–61*

Planing, *pages 62–71*

Chiseling, *pages 72–75*

Routing, *pages 76–81*

Drilling and hammering, *pages 82–85*

Gluing and clamping, *pages 106–107*

◄ ▼ **Through mortise-and-tenon**
A through mortise-and-tenon offers maximum strength, because the tongue extends to the full depth of the mouth.

▼ ▶ **Stopped mortise-and-tenon**
The tongue of a stopped mortise-and-tenon (also known as a stub mortise-and-tenon) penetrates to about two-thirds the width of the wood. This joint is often used in furniture-making, so that the end grain of the tenon is not visible on the outside of table and chair legs.

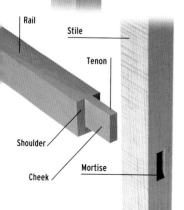

Rail

Stile

Tenon

Shoulder

Mortise

Cheek

Length of tenon equals two-thirds width of stile

Depth of mortise equals two-thirds width of stile

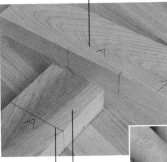

Stile (mortise piece)

Shoulder line | Rail (tenon piece)

Marking a through mortise-and-tenon

◀ **1** Cut the boards to size and plane them square. Mark the shoulder lines on the rail (tenon piece) to correspond with the width of the stile (mortise piece). Mark two lines across the edge of the stile to correspond with the width of the tenon. Code the matching pieces for clarity.

▶ **2** Use a try square to extend the marks across to the other edge of the stile.

▼ **3** Set the pins of a mortise gauge to match the width of the mortise chisel, which should be about one-third the thickness of the wood. In this case, the wood is ³/₄ in. (18mm) thick and a ¹/₄-in. (6mm) mortise chisel is used.

◀ **4** Mark the mortise, setting the stock of the gauge so that the pins centralize across the thickness of the wood. Shade the waste area.

Marking a stopped mortise-and-tenon

Mark the components of a stopped mortise-and-tenon in the same way as a through joint, but this time make the length of the tenon equal to about two-thirds the width of the stile. Mark the mortise on one edge of the stile only; there is no need to carry these marks across to the other edge.

◀ **5** Use the gauge with the same width setting to mark a pair of continuous lines centrally around the edges and end of the tenon piece. Shade the waste area.

Cutting a through mortise

◄ **6** Clamp the wood on edge firmly on the bench. The best way to do this is to place a piece of scrapwood in the vise, and then clamp the mortise piece to the scrapwood so that it is supported on the bench. Using a mortise chisel and mallet, make a series of fine cuts at ⅛-in. (3mm) intervals from the center toward each end. Use a try square to guide the alignment of the chisel.

► **7** A waste portion is needed for levering out the chips, so do not chisel right up to the lines.

► **8** Carefully lever out the chips, letting the chisel pivot on the remaining waste area to do so. Repeat this process in staged depths. After you have cut through to about halfway, reverse the wood and repeat the action from the other side.

Cutting a stopped mortise

Place the chisel against the rail (tenon piece), aligning the end of the chisel with the shoulder line of the tenon, and wrap a piece of masking tape around the blade as a depth guide, so that you do not cut the mortise too deep. If using power tools, set the depth of cut accordingly.

▼ **9** Carefully chisel the end and side walls of the mortise vertically; use a try square to align the cut. It is important that they are flat and square.

Power-tool alternatives

▶ **Hollow chisel mortiser:** Use a hollow chisel mortiser to remove the waste from the mortise by cutting a series of square holes. The inner bit cuts the hole, while the chisel housing is pressed into the wood to make the hole clean and square-edged. Cut to the full depth in one pass, making sure that the bit aligns perfectly to the gauge lines.

◀ ▼ **Drill and drill stand:** Use an ordinary drill in a drill stand, or a drill press, to drill out the waste. Choose a bit that is slightly narrower than the required mortise. Drill the end holes first, then eliminate the waste by working in toward the center. Use a chisel to pare the edges of the mortise square.

▶ **Router:** Use a router to cut accurate mortises, in the same way as you would cut a groove or dado. Choose a bit diameter that matches the required width of mortise. If the stile is too narrow to work with the fence on your router, sandwich the stile between two pieces of scrapwood. The router will produce a mortise with rounded ends, so either square up the corners with a chisel, or take the easier option of rounding the corners of the tenon with a rasp or file and then sandpaper (see page 88).

Mortise with rounded ends

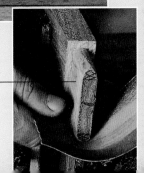

Use sandpaper to round the ends of the tenon.

Cutting a tenon

◄ **10** Mount the tenon piece upright in the vise and use a tenon saw to cut away the cheeks. Alternatively, tilt the wood away from you at a 45-degree angle so that you can see two guidelines at the same time. Saw down to the shoulder line on both scribed lines, then turn the wood around and repeat on the other side.

Finish by mounting the wood upright and sawing horizontally down to the shoulder line.

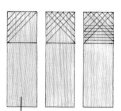

Angle of vertical saw cuts when wood is tilted in the vise.

► **11** Using either the vise or a bench hook, saw the tenon cheeks across the grain at the shoulder line. You can also use a router or machine saw to cut the tenon, by adapting the techniques used for cutting a rabbet.

Assembling the joint

► **12** Carefully drive the joint home using a mallet, or a hammer with scrapwood. If it is too tight, take the joint apart and pare the sticking points with a chisel. Glue and clamp; when dry, clean up the joint with a hand plane.

Broken tenon

Loose tenon

Fixing a loose or broken tenon

■ If you have cut a loose tenon, a quick repair is to pack the joint with thin shims. Use a chisel to cut tapered slivers of matching wood. Squirt glue into the gaps, and slide the wedges in until they are tight.

■ If a tenon breaks off, trim it back level with the shoulder line, and then cut a slot in the end of the rail. Cut and trim a loose tenon to fit both the slot and the mortise, and glue it in place.

Reinforced mortise-and-tenons

The tenon in the previous step-by-step sequence has two shoulders, one on each face of the wood. There is a risk that the mortise will be visible if it is cut overlong by mistake. The addition of a third shoulder on one edge of the tenon moves the joint components away from a frame corner, so that both mortise and tenon are enclosed by wood in the joint. Edge shoulders can be haunched for greater strength. When adding an edge shoulder, remember to adjust the mortise accordingly.

Cutting an edge shoulder

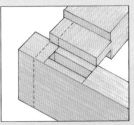

▲ **1** Cut the face shoulders, then align the tenon to the mortise and mark the cutting line for the edge shoulder.

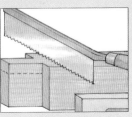

▲ **2** Saw off the waste, being careful not to saw into the face shoulders.

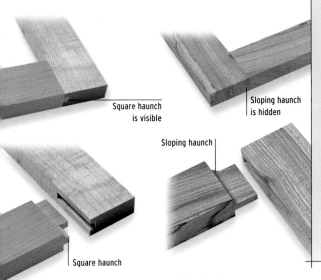

Square haunch is visible

Sloping haunch is hidden

Sloping haunch

Square haunch

▲ Haunched mortise-and-tenons

The addition of an edge shoulder strengthens resistance to racking (distortion due to sideways pressure), but it also increases the risk of the tenon twisting. A small tongue, known as a haunch, can be added to combat this. A square haunch will be visible after assembly; a sloping haunch will be hidden. Haunched mortise-and-tenons are used at the corners of frames.

▼ Wedged mortise-and-tenon

To tighten or splay the tenon so that it cannot be withdrawn, through tenons can be slotted to receive wedges; these force the tenon to form a dovetail. The mortise is sometimes tapered wider on the side opposite insertion. The same technique can be used on a stopped joint, but the wedges (called foxtail wedges) must be cut precisely to fit, because the joint cannot be disassembled.

Drilled holes

Saw cuts

Wedges

Dovetail joints

Considered the hallmark of fine craftsmanship, dovetails provide both mechanical strength and visual appeal. They can be made by hand or machine; dovetail jigs are available for the router. All types of dovetail joint depend upon the wedge shape for strength; the through dovetail is demonstrated here.

SEE ALSO
Holding and clamping, *pages 24–25*

Measuring and marking, *pages 32–41*

Sawing, *pages 42–61*

Planing, *pages 62–71*

Chiseling, *pages 72–75*

Routing, *pages 76–81*

Gluing and clamping, *pages 106–107*

Dovetail angles and jigs

For optimum strength, a 1:6 angle is used for softwoods and a 1:8 angle for hardwoods. You can buy dovetail templates, but they are easy to make.

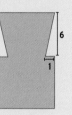

Hardwood angle   Softwood angle

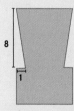

To mark out a dovetail angle, butt a sliding bevel to the edge of the wood. Set the angle by aligning the blade 6 (or 8) units up and 1 unit across.

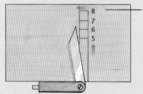

A scrapwood jig cut at the dovetail angle with stops at each end, to aid marking and guarantee that angles are consistent.

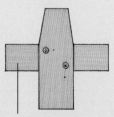

This jig includes the dovetail angle, and can also be used to square the lines across the wood.

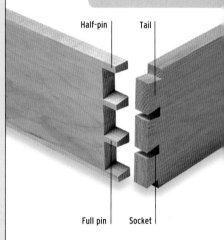

Half-pin | Tail

Full pin | Socket

Dovetail terminology

Tails: Angled like a dove's tail when viewed from the face of the board, these are drawn straight across the end grain with a try square.

Pins: These are angled across the end grain, with their wider ends toward the inside face of the board.

Half-pins: The name comes from the fact that they are angled on only one side, not that they are half the size of the other pins.

▲ Through dovetail

When used to join a drawer back to the sides, the pin piece forms the back and the tail piece forms the side.

Marking the tail piece

▶ **1** Cut the boards to size and plane them square. Using a try square, mark light shoulder lines all the way around both pieces. The depth of the shoulder line should equal the thickness of the wood.

◀ **2** Using a sliding bevel or a dovetail template and pencil, mark the positions of the tails on one board.

Dovetail positions

■ The size and spacing of the pins and tails can vary, but regular spacing usually looks best. As a general guide, the widest end of the tails is usually about two or three times the narrowest end of the pins—for example, ³/₄-in. (9mm) tails and ¹/₄-in. (6mm) pins.

■ To mark out evenly spaced tails on the end grain of a board, measure and mark ¹/₄ in. (6mm) in from each edge of the board. Divide the distance between these marks equally for the number of tails required; mark these points. Measure and mark ¹/₈ in. (3mm) on either side of these points; this is the spacing between each tail.

▼ **3** Using a try square, square the lines across the end of the wood. Shade the waste areas.

Cutting the tail piece

◄ **4** Secure the wood in a vise and tilt it at an angle so that the left sides of all the tails are vertical. You will find this aids accurate cutting, because gravity naturally pushes the saw down. Use a dovetail saw to cut them, making sure that you saw on the waste side of each line. Tilt the wood so that the right sides of all the dovetails are vertical, and saw those.

► **5** Using a try square and marking knife, deepen the shoulder line on the waste areas that are to be cut away. Remove the end waste with the dovetail saw, working across the grain carefully to the line.

► **6** Remove the waste between the dovetails with a coping saw, cutting to about 1/8 in. (3mm) from the shoulder line. The 1/8 in. (3mm) is left on at this stage, because it can only be removed accurately with a very sharp chisel.

▼ **8** Mount the wood back in the vise and clean up the shoulder lines with the chisel.

◄ **7** With a piece of scrapwood underneath the board, chisel back to the shoulder line; use a series of fine vertical cuts to half the thickness of the wood, then turn the wood over to cut from the other side. This will prevent the wood fibers from splitting or breaking out.

Marking and cutting the pin piece

◀ **9** Mount the second piece of wood in the vise. Place a piece of scrapwood on the bench top, and raise the second board in the vise so that the end of it is level with the top of the scrapwood. Place the first piece (with tails cut) across them, making sure that it lies flat. Align the shoulder lines and edges perfectly. Mark around the tails.

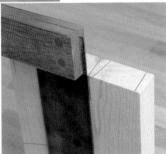

▼ **11** Carefully use the dovetail saw to cut on the waste side of the lines, down the grain to the shoulder line. As before, use a coping saw to remove the waste nearly to the line. Be careful not to cut into the angled pins.

▶ **10** Using a try square, extend the lines down the front of the joint. Shade the waste areas.

▼ **12** Deepen the cut on the shoulder line to define it clearly, then carefully chisel back to the shoulder line, overlapping each chisel cut to maintain a straight line. A narrow chisel gives much better control.

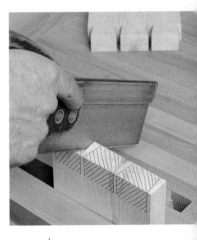

▼ **13** Place the wood in the vise so that you can chisel horizontally to clean up the shoulder line. Take care not to cut right across or you will split the fibers.

Pins or tails first?

In this demonstration, the tails are cut first and then used to mark the pins on the second board. However, you can start with the pins first if you prefer.

Assembling the joint

◀ **14** Partially assemble the joint to check that the pieces fit together well. Do not drive the joint fully home at this stage; just tap the pieces together for about ⅛ in. (3mm). Use a chisel to make any necessary adjustments to achieve a good fit.

▶ **15** When everything fits together well, coat the matching surfaces with glue and clamp together. You can use a shaped block of scrapwood to help squeeze the dovetails up to the shoulder line of the matching piece, as well as to prevent bruising from the clamp. Check that the joint is square with a try square.

◀ **16** When the glue has dried, clean up the joint with a plane, working inward to avoid splitting the end grain on the joint itself. The edges can be planed diagonally to tidy them up, holding the wood in the vise.

Through dovetail variations

■ **Drawer dovetail:** The layout of through dovetails on drawers allows the bottom groove to run out under a tail and through a pin where the open groove on the drawer's side is plugged.

■ **Miter dovetail:** In the layout for this joint, the half-pin is inset from the edge, and one side of the half-pin is not sawn; instead, the extra material beyond it is mitered.

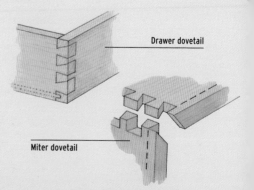

Drawer dovetail

Miter dovetail

Using a router and dovetail jig

◀ **1** Dovetail jigs for the router can be used to cut both the pins and tails. Read the manufacturer's manual for how to set up the particular jig that you are using. Here, the jig has been set up in the mode for cutting pins; the router is used with a straight bit to rout out the waste.

▶ **2** Here, the jig has been reversed and set up in the mode for cutting tails; the router is used with a dovetail bit to rout out the waste. After a little practice, the jig can be finetuned to such a degree that finished dovetails will squeeze together by hand without any gaps showing. Glue and clamp as for a handcut dovetail.

Veneering a loose dovetail

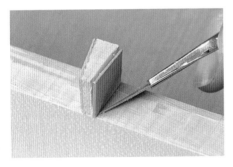

◀ **1** If you have cut a loose dovetail—for example, if you cut on the wrong side of the marked cutting line—the joint will be loose by the thickness of the line. A quick remedy is to use strips of veneer. Study the joint, and decide whether the pins or the tails are at fault. Glue strips of matching veneer to the affected pieces, then assemble the joint.

▶ **2** Alternatively, glue and assemble the joint, then apply glue to the strips of veneer and slide them into the loose joint. Use a gap-filling glue if the mistake is serious. For both methods, use a chisel to pare the veneer ends level.

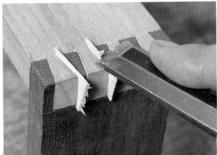

4
Specialist techniques

An introduction to shaping, bending, veneering, carving and turning techniques

Shaping and bending

When a board is sawn and planed, it becomes straight. It takes time to produce shapes and curves, but they can add great interest to a project. Shaped components can be cut from solid wood, or created using techniques such as brick construction, stack laminating or coopering. Wood can also be bent into shape, using techniques such as kerfing, bending laminates around a form or steam bending. Shaping and bending techniques are often used in chairmaking, as well as for woodcarving. Detailed drawings are essential, and for more complicated shapes, it may be a good idea to make a rough model first from an easily shaped material, such as balsa wood or plaster of Paris. This way, you will be able to see the form from all angles to be sure that you are achieving the desired shape.

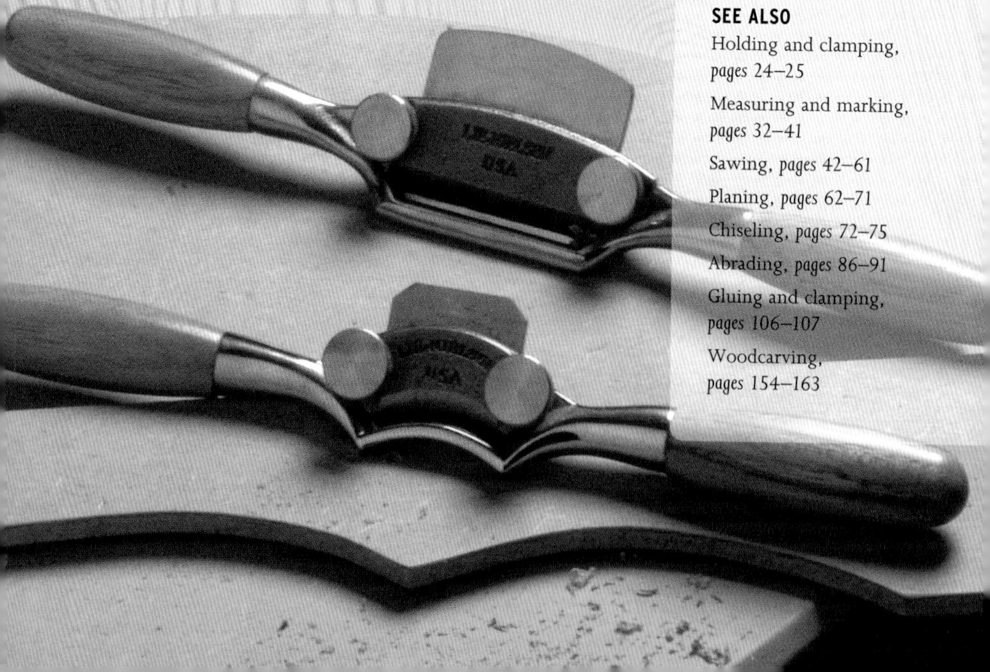

SEE ALSO

Holding and clamping, pages 24–25

Measuring and marking, pages 32–41

Sawing, pages 42–61

Planing, pages 62–71

Chiseling, pages 72–75

Abrading, pages 86–91

Gluing and clamping, pages 106–107

Woodcarving, pages 154–163

Cutting curves

Most curves in woodwork are imposed onto the grain and do not always follow it, but you still have to observe the nature of the grain to obtain adequate strength. Many shaped components, such as a stool or table leg, can simply be cut from a single piece of solid wood. However, where a curve results in short grain, the wood will be weaker and more liable to break than where the length of the grain is utilized. Keep this in mind when planning a project. You may need to attach an extra piece of wood with glue, screws or dowels to overcome the problem.

Grain strength

In this hoop with the grain running vertically, the checks indicate adequate grain strength and the crosses indicate weak or short grain. When introducing curves in a piece of woodwork, try to avoid short grain, because the wood is likely to break along it.

Cutting and carving

◀ 1 To cut a curved stool or table leg, mark the shape of the leg on two adjacent surfaces and on both ends (in the same way as when carving in the round). Saw the piece roughly to shape; a bandsaw is ideal, but a jigsaw or coping saw can also be used.

▶ 2 Hold the leg in a vise or clamp it to the bench, then shape with a spokeshave or carving gouge. Hold the gouge like a chisel, and pare away the fibers in the direction of the grain. For even finer shaping, use carving rasps and then sandpaper.

▲ Glued curves

A simple way to add a curve at the end of a straight piece is to glue on an extra piece; make sure that the grain matches. The shaded portion and cutaway section show the intended shape.

Constructing curves

To avoid the problems of weak short grain, you can construct larger curved pieces from smaller curved elements. Brick construction and stack laminating have numerous applications, such as to create curves for bowed drawer fronts that are veneered afterward. Traditional coopering is the process of making curved casks from staves of wood, but the technique can also be used to create shapes for other projects, by forming part or whole circles from identical segments.

Brick construction

◀ **1** Draw the required curved segment (or segments) on paper, then trace or transfer the data onto a piece of wood to act as a template for marking all the brick pieces. Cut the pieces on a bandsaw, or use a jigsaw or coping saw. The more accurate you are in sawing to the line, the less trimming you will need to do afterward to finish the curve evenly.

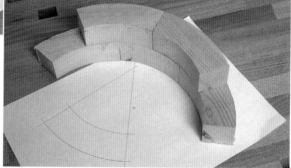

▶ **2** Build the shape one layer at a time, staggering the bricks in the same way as when building a brick wall. Glue the bricks together using a rubbed glue joint (see page 113); clamp if you feel it is necessary.

Positioning the bricks

Make a full-size drawing of the shape you want to form. From this, you can decide on the best positioning of the brick courses to achieve a strong structure.

▶ Stack laminating

This technique involves gluing identically shaped pieces of wood vertically. Cut the pieces in the same way as for brick construction.

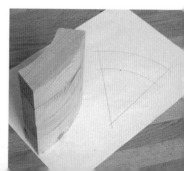

Coopering

▶ 1 To make a coopered circle, draw two concentric circles on paper and divide them into equal-sized segments. Convert the curved sides of the segment shape into flat sides. Using a steel rule and sliding bevel, transfer the segment dimensions onto a length of wood. Saw the required number of segments, taking care to cut the angles accurately.

◀ 2 Glue the segments together to form a circle; a rubbed glue joint should suffice, without the need for clamping (see page 113). Allow the segments to dry on a flat papered surface to prevent them from sticking to the bench. When dry, mark a circular line around the outside edge. Trim the wood to the line. You can do this by a variety of means, such as chiseling or sanding.

▶ 3 Another method is to use a plane; rotate the wood in a vise, keeping the plane more or less horizontal.

◀ 4 Finish the inner curve. Here, coarse sandpaper is wrapped around a curved stick to make sanding easier.

Kerfing

This technique involves making a series of saw cuts (kerfs) partially through the wood, so that the remaining material is capable of bending. Kerfing offers very little strength, because most of the fibers are cut through, so it is only suitable for nonloadbearing applications. Kerfing by hand is laborious, but is easy with a machine saw; two types of machine saw are demonstrated here.

Calculating kerf spacing

Make a full-size drawing and measure the length of the curve on its outer face. On the wood, mark the point at which the bending will start and saw a kerf here, leaving at least $\frac{1}{8}$ in. (3mm) of wood unsawn. Measure and mark the length of the curve from this first kerf. Clamp the kerfed end of the wood to the bench, then lift the free end until the kerf closes. Wedge the free end in position at this point. Measure the distance between the bench and the underside of the board. This is the distance between kerfs.

Cutting the kerfs

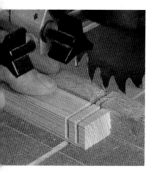

◀ **1** Mark the kerf spacing on the fence of a radial-arm saw the required distance from the saw blade. Set the depth of cut and make a series of cuts partially through the wood, moving the wood each time to align the previous cut with the kerf-spacing mark on the fence.

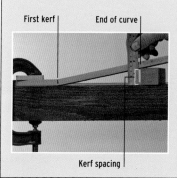

First kerf | End of curve

Kerf spacing

▶ **2** On a bandsaw, clamp a straight batten to the saw table, so that the blade is half buried in a saw cut on the batten. The batten will act as a depth stop, as well as a marker for the kerf spacing.

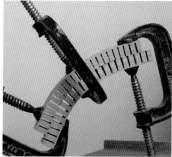

▶ **3** Test that the wood bends as required, then apply glue to each kerf; bend into shape and clamp. A strip of veneer glued along the kerfed side will strengthen it. You can also glue and clamp two pieces together with their kerfs inward.

Bending laminates

Numerous thin strips (laminations) of wood—each strip up to ⅛ in. (3mm) thick—can be glued together and bent around a form, usually a male and female mold. The terms male and female refer to convex and concave shapes that usually match. The grain follows the length of the strips, and the resulting structures are very strong. Cheaper constructional veneers can be sandwiched between decorative facing veneers.

Using a form

▶ **1** Construct a male and female mold, allowing for the thickness of the laminated structure. Cut some laminates slightly larger than required, and make a trial run, bending and clamping them without glue.

◀ **2** Apply glue to each face of the laminates, then clamp them between the molds; tighten the clamps from the center outward. Use sheets of waxed paper or plastic to prevent the laminates from sticking to the molds. When dry, remove from the molds and trim the edges with a plane.

Making molds

Make a full-size drawing of the shape, and use this to help you make accurate male and female molds using particle board, MDF or solid wood. You need to allow for the thickness of the entire laminated structure, which means that the curves of each mold will follow different radii.

▶ **Freeform shaping**

You can bend laminates (or even thin solid wood) without a form, and improvise a jig to hold the piece in place after gluing. Here, a piece of thin plywood has been twisted and clamped to a length of thicker wood to hold it in the twisted position.

Steam bending

Wood is more pliable when it is wet or hot. Steam bending involves putting the wood into a sealed chamber that is filled with steam from a constant source; on a small scale, you could use a stove kettle or pressure cooker to generate the steam. When the wood is saturated, it is taken out and bent around a form. The method is hit or miss, because the final bend may straighten out slightly when dry, and bends that are too tight can break.

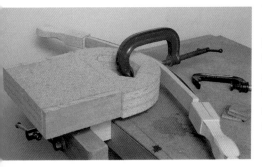

Using a steam chamber

◀ **1** Build a form using plywood, particle board or MDF; it must offer some places where clamps can be located. Make a bending strap from thin sheet steel; attach it to wooden handles and hardwood end stops with bolts and screws. Make the distance between the end stops the same as the length of the wood being bent. Do a trial run without bending the wood.

Bending tips

■ Thin wood bends more easily than thick wood. It is rare for wood thicker than about 1³/₈ in. (35mm) to be steam bent, although 2 in. (50mm) has been achieved in industrial production. Even then, a percentage of tight bends break.

■ Some woods are more bendy than others. Ash, beech and yew, for example, yield more easily than mahogany or teak.

▶ **2** Prepare the steam generator, such as a pressure cooker, and the steam chamber; for example, an insulated plywood box or piece of plastic drainpipe plugged at both ends with wooden disks, with a rubber tube to carry the steam.

◀ **3** In this example, a drainpipe is insulated with aluminum foil and fiberglass roof insulation. The chamber is mounted at a slight downward slant, so that condensed water can escape from the end into a bucket.

◀ **4** Stack the wood to be bent into the tube, separating it with spacers to allow the steam to circulate around it. Replace the wooden disk and switch on the steam generator. As a general rule, wood needs one hour of steaming for every 1 in. (25mm) of thickness.

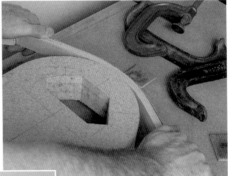

▶ **5** After steaming, quickly place the wood along the metal strap and bend it around the form; you may need to wear thick gloves to prevent scalding. Some trial and error is required to get it right. The steel strap helps to prevent fiber breakout.

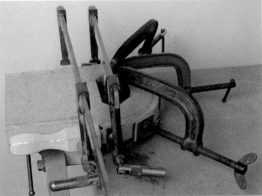

◀ **6** Secure the strap to the form with clamps and allow to dry for several days.

▶ Microwave bending

You can use a microwave oven to heat small sections of wood instead of steaming it. It helps to keep the wood moist by placing it in a strong, sealed plastic bag with a little water in it, or by wrapping it in a saturated cloth. Set the microwave oven at its highest temperature and microwave for 3–5 minutes for bending $\frac{1}{8}$-in. (3mm) thick wood. After microwaving, quickly place the wood in the form and clamp; allow to dry out fully for a few hours.

Veneering

A veneer is a wafer-thin piece of the tree that can be glued onto a solid wood or manmade board groundwork, the latter being more stable and without the problems of wood movement associated with solid wood constructions. Veneers are thin and flexible, so they can be applied both to flat and curved surfaces. Veneering is an extremely efficient way of utilizing wood, because it gives you a great deal more wood species to choose from and is relatively inexpensive. Also, by restricting some rare species of wood for veneer cutting only, it has conserved those species or at least extended their life.

SEE ALSO

Veneers and inlays,
page 18

Holding and clamping,
pages 24–25

Measuring and marking,
pages 32–41

Planing, pages 62–71

Chiseling, pages 72–75

Routing, pages 76–81

Abrading, pages 86–91

Gluing and clamping,
pages 106–107

Shaping and bending,
pages 140–147

Applying veneers

The front of the veneer is called the closed face; the back is called the open face. If you flex the veneer along the grain, you will find that it bends more when the open face is convex—an easy way of identifying the faces if you are unsure. It is a good idea to number veneers in sequence, because it can be difficult to match them if they get out of order. Veneers are applied to the groundwork using glue and pressure.

Preparation and cutting

◀ **1** Make sure that the groundwork is smooth and free from dust—any defects will remain visible beneath the veneer. If necessary, flatten the veneer by dampening both sides, then clamping it between two boards for a few hours. Select a piece of veneer slightly larger than the groundwork; it will be trimmed precisely to size after application. Use veneer tape (see page 152) to bind any splits in the veneer by taping the outer side. Support the veneer on a backing board, place the groundwork on top and mark around the perimeter.

▶ **2** Using a steel rule and marking knife, carefully cut the veneer about ⅛ in. (3mm) outside the marked line. It is important to cut across the grain first, because this is most likely to split. By using the marking knife at a shallow angle, with the index finger applying pressure, the action is firm and slow, especially at the end of the cut where the grain is likely to break out. The blade at this point is almost horizontal.

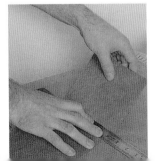

◀ **3** Another method involves cutting halfway through with a marking knife, and then breaking the fibers by lifting the veneer against a steel rule for a clean cut.

Caul veneering

▶ **1** This technique involves clamping the glued elements against a caul, or between a pair of cauls. The cauls may be flat or shaped (like the forms used for bending laminates). Place the groundwork on top of a sheet of paper, then apply the glue with a roller, spatula or brush.

▼ **2** Allow the glue to dry for a few minutes so that the water evaporates, then place the oversize veneer on top of the groundwork. This prevents glue stains from coming through the veneer, or excessive water from buckling it, which is still possible even when clamped.

◀ **3** Mount the veneered panel against the caul and clamp so that the pressure is even. Allow to dry overnight or for at least two hours under pressure at 60°F (15°C).

▼ **4** When dry, trim the veneer with a marking knife against a backing board. Tilt the panel with a spacer to transfer pressure to the knife cut. The veneered panel is now ready for sanding.

Other application techniques

■ **Hammer veneering:** This traditional method uses heated hide (animal) glue and a special veneer hammer to apply pressure. This is a very skilled technique, and is usually limited to restoration or reproduction work.

■ **Vacuum veneering:** Portable vacuum presses are now available for the home woodworker for an easy-to-achieve professional result. The glued elements are placed inside a vacuum bag; a vacuum pump then removes the air from the bag. This creates sufficient atmospheric pressure uniformly over the piece to bond the veneer to the groundwork.

■ **Special glues:** These include contact glues that stick on impact, and iron-on glues that are pressed with a domestic hot iron. Some veneers are available coated with a pressure-sensitive adhesive that sticks on impact.

Repairing veneers

▼ 1 If an air pocket gets trapped under the veneer, use a knife to split the blister along the grain. Use the blade and a slip of paper to work as much glue as possible between the veneer and groundwork. Wipe away any excess glue,

place a piece of wet wax paper on top of the glued area, then clamp until the glue dries. You can use the same technique to repair lifts at the edges of the veneer.

► 2 To replace a damaged area, tape a piece of matching veneer on top so that the grain is aligned. Cut through the double layer and down to the groundwork. Use a chisel to pare the groundwork to a smooth finish, then glue in the veneer patch.

Veneering tips

■ When veneering solid-wood groundwork, it is best to veneer both sides, even if only one side will be visible. This balances the way the wood reacts and moves as the glue and veneer dry, and when there are changes in moisture and humidity levels. You can use a cheaper veneer for the side that will not be seen.

■ When using solid-wood groundwork, match the grain direction of the veneer to the groundwork, so that they move together when there are changes in moisture and humidity levels.

■ On plywood, place the veneer at 90 degrees to the grain of the plywood.

Edging strip

▼ 1 A small solid wood edging strip can be used to strengthen two adjacent veneered surfaces; an edging strip in a contrasting wood can also add visual interest. Use a router with a fence and straight bit to rout a small rabbet around the edge to accommodate the edging strip.

◄ 2 On straight or gentle curves, simply glue the edging strip in place and use masking tape to hold the pieces together. For more severe curves, bend the edging strip first (such as by microwave bending). Once the glue has set, remove the tape. Sand the edging or scrape it level with the veneer.

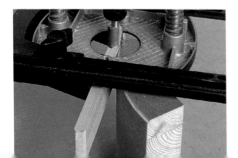

Decorative veneer effects

Interesting effects can be produced by cutting and laying veneers to create a pattern. Here, a small panel is diamond-matched and edged with cross banding. An oval motif is inlaid into the center, and the banding is highlighted with decorative stringing. Decorative inlays can be purchased in a variety of shapes, sizes and patterns.

Diamond-matching

▶ **1** Diamond-matching works best with straight-grained veneer, and involves cutting four equal quadrants of veneer with the grain running diagonally. Cut the first quadrant, using a marking knife and backing board, and use this piece as a template for the others.

▼ **2** Place the four pieces of veneer together so that their grain forms a diamond pattern. Join the pieces using veneer tape; also tape any splits.

Inlay motif

◀ **3** Position the inlay motif, with the protective paper overlay uppermost, onto the center of the veneer panel; draw pencil guidelines to help you align it.

▶ **4** Use a marking knife to cut through the veneer around the motif. Fit the motif inside the opening and tape it down. Glue the prepared veneer panel to the groundwork in the usual way.

In this example, the groundwork is larger than the veneer panel to accommodate a border; use a cutting gauge to trim the edges of the veneer parallel to the edges of the groundwork.

Veneer tape

This gummed paper tape is used to join pieces of veneer together and to bind any splits in the veneer. Moisten the tape (you can lick it), and apply it to the outer face of the veneer. As the tape dries, it shrinks and pulls the edges of the joint or split together. The tape can be dampened and scraped from the veneer after the veneer has been glued to the groundwork.

Cross banding

◀ **5** Prepare the cross-banding border by cutting strips of veneer with the grain running across their width rather than length for decorative effect; join the strips with tape where necessary to achieve the desired lengths. Cut miters at the corners by laying the strips in situ and carefully cutting through both together. Glue the border to the groundwork using veneer tape and cauls.

Stringing

▶ **6** Stringings are narrow strips of veneer in varying patterns of short-grained wood sections. Use a router with a straight fence to rout a very fine groove around the panel, between the diamond-matched section and the border. Take great care when using narrow bits, because they are very fragile.

▶ **7** Straighten the radiused corners of the routed grooves with a chisel. Carefully cut the stringings by marking the mitered joints with the chisel, then cut the stringings to the marked line against a backing board. Use a spatula or brush to apply a little glue into the grooves, and carefully inset the stringings. A pin hammer can be used to press the stringings into place.

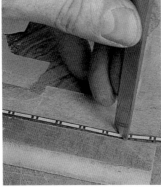

Marquetry and parquetry

Marquetry is a decorative design, picture or pattern formed from veneers. Parquetry is a decorative design formed from geometric shapes.

Finishing

◀ **8** Clean up the panel using a cabinet scraper. First, moisten the veneer tape with a damp cloth, and then scrape away the tape to reveal the beauty of the wood beneath. Take care to work with the grain or diagonally to maintain a smooth cut. Although veneer is very thin, it is remarkable how it stands up to being scraped.

Woodcarving

Carving in wood is a combination of both art and craft. Wood can be carved into utilitarian objects, such as bowls, boxes and spoons, or into forms purely for aesthetic pleasure, such as abstract sculptures. The craft of carving is the acquired skill of removing the unwanted wood efficiently. The art of carving is in the design—a carving should be satisfying to look at, pleasing to touch and, if it is a functional object, it should be well adapted to its purpose. There are two main categories of woodcarving—relief carving and carving in the round.

SEE ALSO

Holding and clamping, pages 24–25

Measuring and marking, pages 32–41

Sawing, pages 42–61

Chiseling, pages 72–75

Abrading, pages 86–91

Tool maintenance, pages 92–99

Carving tools

It is possible to do a great deal of woodcarving with relatively few tools, and your particular needs will vary according to your style, preferred subjects and the scale of the work you do. The tools that all carvers need are chisels, gouges and a mallet. They come in a wide selection of shapes and sizes.

▶ Chisels and gouges

Unlike standard chisels and gouges, carvers' tools have a bevel on both sides of the blade, allowing them to cut wood at a variety of angles. Chisels have flat cross-sections; gouges are curved. A veiner is a deep U-shaped gouge; a parting (or V) tool is a V-shaped gouge; a skew chisel has an angled edge for cutting into corners. Different numbering systems are used to identify the shape of the cutting edge; most are available in a variety of widths. Start with larger tools for rough carving, then progress to smaller ones for refining work. The tools and handles can be bought separately, but ask the supplier to fit your chosen handle, because it must be put on straight.

From top to bottom: Straight chisel, skew chisel, straight gouge, parting tool and veiner.

◀ Mallet

This round-headed mallet allows you to change the direction of a stroke rapidly without worrying about how the face of the mallet is angled to the tool. The handle has a swelling at the end so that you can work with a loose grip. Mallets are available in different sizes, weights and materials; choose the one that feels best to you.

▶ Rasps, rifflers and files

These abrasive tools can be useful for removing stock quickly. Rasps make a more aggressive cut; rifflers are small, shaped rasps; files are a fine type of rasp. They can be used in any grain direction.

Rasp

Riffler

Blade shapes

All gouges are designed to make a curved cut. When gouges are defined as being straight, curved, bent, spoon and so on, this describes the shape of the blade along its length—for example, straight gouges have sides that are parallel along most of the shank, while spoon gouges have a straight shank with a deeply curved tip. Each tool is designed to do a specific task—to reach, dig, scoop or pare.

Spoon gouge

Preparing to carve

The chisels and gouges used for carving must be very sharp. Although the sharpening procedure is essentially the same as for standard woodworking tools, there are a few crucial differences. It is also important that the piece being carved is held securely on the workbench, so that both hands are left free for carving.

◀ Sharpening chisels

Use the same sharpening procedure as for standard woodworking chisels. However, whereas the standard tools have a primary ground bevel plus a secondary honed bevel, carver's chisels only have a single bevel angle. Make sure that you maintain this angle when sharpening. Another difference is that carver's chisels are beveled on both the upper and underside of the cutting edge; the bevel needs to be sharpened on both sides.

▶ Sharpening parting tools

Parting (V-shaped) tools are the most awkward to sharpen. Treat them as two separate chisels, then remove the hook-shaped point by rocking the V as though it were a tiny gouge. Use a slipstone to sharpen the inside edge.

Sharpening gouges

▲ 1 Carvers' gouges normally have a bevel on the inside, as well as a larger bevel on the outside. When sharpening the outer bevel, rock the tool back and forth as you move it across the sharpening stone; this will sharpen the entire bevel evenly.

▶ 2 Sharpen the inner bevel with a slipstone, rocking it slightly to curve the bevel. Take care not to remove the corners when sharpening a gouge.

Holding the work

▶ **1** The holding device will vary according to the type of work, and you will need to improvise. Here, a small stop is screwed parallel with the tapered edge of a wedge. When the wedge is tapped in, the panel is forced against the long stop on the other side.

◀ **2** A special carver's vise allows you to swivel the work, and can be moved anywhere on the workbench. It is also made largely of wood, which reduces the risk of damage to chisels if they slip.

▼ **3** A carver's turntable allows you to turn the work around to view it from any angle. Screw the feet of the turntable to the bench, and screw or clamp the work to the table.

▼ ▶ **4** A carver's bench screw passes through the workbench and is screwed into the base or back of the carving, with the nut tightened on the underside of the bench.

Two types of bench screw

Choice of wood

■ Some woods are better for carving than others, but it is worth trying any wood that is available. If your carving is to be elaborate and you plan to give it a natural finish, it is better to avoid wood with a pronounced grain pattern, which can make the carving difficult to see. In a simple, bold form, on the other hand, the grain of the wood can contribute to the final effect.

■ The purpose of the carving may be significant in your choice of wood. If you are making a salad bowl, for example, avoid yew, which is poisonous; also avoid softwoods, such as cedar, that have a strong taste. Instead, choose a hardwood such as sycamore or poplar. For a purely decorative object, color and grain might be the governing factors in your choice.

Tool cuts

Straight chisels and gouges are strong tools that are used to do most of the heavy work. They are held in both hands and pushed, or held in one hand and struck with a mallet; gentle use of a mallet gives more control than pushing. There are times when a mallet is essential; for example, in the initial stages when roughing out, it is quicker to remove large amounts of waste with a gouge and mallet than with just your hands and a gouge. Bent, curved and spoon gouges are generally pushed and levered.

Using a mallet

◄ 1 Use one hand to guide the tool, while the other strikes with the mallet. Start with the tool at a steep angle, so that it bites into the wood. The idea is not to make big heavy blows, but rather to tap-tap-tap with the mallet.

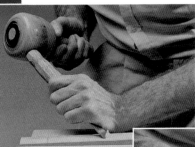

◄ 2 Make a scooping action by bringing the tool's handle down in an arc as the blade moves forward. The quicker the movement, the sharper the curve; a slow action makes a gentler curve.

▶ 3 It is important to continue the scooping action for the whole arc, especially when removing a lot of waste, because if you drive forward too far, the gouge can easily become stuck.

◄ Using both hands

A large proportion of carving is done with two hands on the chisel or gouge—one hand pushing hard, the other restraining and guiding the blade.

Stabbing and slicing

◄ ▼ **1** Stab the chisel to the desired depth. To cut a diamond, for example, make four stabs across it so that the chisel is stabbed to the

desired depth at the center of the diamond, but only touches the surface at the outer points. Remove each of the chips with one cut, slicing along the outer line on the surface and aiming to meet the other cuts at both the center and the points.

◄ ▼ **2** You can use the same technique with a gouge. First, stab a series of curved lines. Slide the blade around to make several stabs for curves that are larger than the gouge. Slice out the chips by pushing hard on the

handle of the tool with one hand, and using your other hand to restrain the blade. Without this restraint, the blade could take out more than one chip.

▼ **Parting (V) tool**	▼ **Spoon gouge**	▼ **Bent gouge**
Carve V grooves across the grain before those with the grain. Do not try to go to the full depth in one go; make several cuts, gradually getting deeper.	Use a spoon gouge to shape hollows. Note that you will not be able to see the cutting edge of the gouge clearly.	Bent gouges can get around concave curves where a straight gouge would dig in. It has the capacity to curve the edges of a fairly small concavity.

Relief carving

Woodcarving in relief is the technique of using gouges and chisels to incise, excavate and model the surface of the wood to a relatively shallow depth. Relief carving is referred to as low-relief or high-relief, depending on how deep the carving is. The process involves drawing the design onto the wood, edging it with vertical cuts, making decisions as to the various levels of the design, and then wasting areas in and around it with gouges. Relief carvings are usually designed to be seen front-on, like a picture.

Setting out

◀ **1** Transfer the drawing onto the wood. You can use carbon paper to trace it, or prick through the drawing at frequent intervals with a sharp point; join the dots using a pencil.

▶ **2** Use a marking gauge to indicate the depth of the background all the way around the edges of the wood.

Grounding in

▼ **3** Remove as much waste wood as you can, using a saw if practicable. Alternatively, use a parting tool to cut around the design, and then gouge out the waste. Keep well outside all the guidelines, only cutting to within about ⅛ in. (3mm) of them.

Basic procedures

The main techniques of relief carving are:

- **Setting out:** Transferring the drawing onto the wood.

- **Grounding in:** Cutting away to the background level.

- **Setting in:** Cutting vertically around the design close to the outline.

- **Bosting:** Roughly shaping the form; also referred to as roughing in or roughing out.

- **Modeling:** Refining and finishing the form.

- **Undercutting:** Working from the front to remove wood under the forms.

A technique is often repeated a number of times during the course of the carving.

Setting in

▶ **4** Begin setting in by using a fairly flat gouge to cut vertically down to the background; keep about 1/8 in. (3mm) away from the outline of the design, and stop at least 1/16 in. (2mm) above the final background level. Ground in to the line you have just set in, using the same gouge.

Chip carving

Chip carving is a shallow-cut technique of making angled cuts to remove small chips and leave V-shaped grooves. Usually done with chip-carving knives, it can also be done with chisels. Chip-carving patterns are usually geometric.

◀ **5** Set in again, close to the line this time, using gouges that match the curves of the design as closely as possible. Keep above the background level. Ground in again, using a wide, fairly flat gouge to remove the wood right down to the background level.

Bosting

▶ **6** Roughly carve the general shapes. Keep redrawing any helpful lines that you remove when carving.

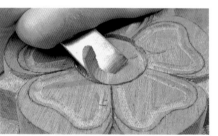

Undercutting

▼ **8** To convey the illusion that the rose is resting on the background and is not part of it, take the curve of the petals around and under. Your angle of attack will vary according to the direction of the grain. Ground in the backgound to its final level.

Modeling

◀ **7** When the bosted shape is well established, start to model and refine all the shapes of the rose. Blend in convex and concave curves.

Carving in the round

Carving in the round, or sculptural carving, is the next developmental step after relief carving. It is a technique in which the carver cuts deeper and deeper into the wood, until the carving is freestanding and can be viewed from all angles. The carver starts by removing as much waste wood as possible using any suitable tool (such as a saw), and then roughs out and models the sculpture using gouges.

Transferring the design and rough cutting

▶ **1** Most woodcarvers start by making drawings and then building a maquette (model) of the image in clay. Use a try square and pencil to trace around the front view of the maquette, then repeat for the side view.

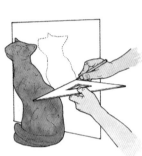

◀ ▼ **2** Transfer the front view onto one side of the wood; leave some extra wood at the bottom for holding in a vise later. Cut out the front-view shape; a bandsaw is ideal for this. Repeat the procedure for the side view. If you are careful, you can tape an offcut from the front view back in place to provide a flat surface to rest on the bandsaw table when cutting the side view.

Transferring side view onto wood

Transferring and rough-cutting process

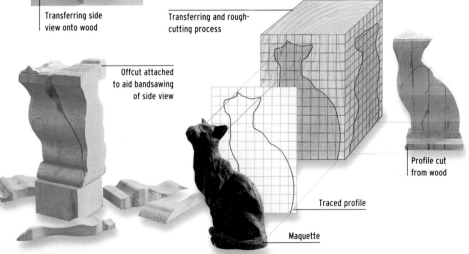

Offcut attached to aid bandsawing of side view

Profile cut from wood

Traced profile

Maquette

◀ **3** Draw some guidelines and general shaping onto the wood at significant places, such as the tops of the shoulders. Indicate the center line on the wood; this will help you to keep the two sides even, and you should redraw any part of it that you carve away.

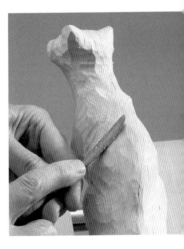

Rough shaping

▶ **4** Set the workpiece in the vise, and use a large flattish gouge to carve what you consider to be the essential form. Try to cut with the grain, from high to low wood.

▶ **5** Make a saw cut into the base block, about ¼ in. (6mm) deep, all the way around just below the tail to enable you to round over the tail and paws.

Sanding carvings

A completed carving can have a tooled or smoothed finish. Sanding takes away the crispness achieved with sharp tools, but this can sometimes be the effect you want. It is important to remember, however, that if you want to recarve a piece that has been sanded, you must wash it first to remove the fine grit that would otherwise blunt your tools.

Modeling

▶ **6** Continue to refine the sculpture using smaller gouge cuts. Alternatively, soften the outlines with rifflers, then smooth with sandpaper, working through the grits. Make sure that all carving is complete before using sandpaper, because particles left in the wood will quickly blunt your tools.

Sanded finish

Gouged finish

◀ **7** Carefully carve in the details, such as eyes and mouth; draw guidelines to help you. Carry out any final finishing, including sawing off the wood from the base.

Woodturning

Turning is one of the simplest techniques in woodworking, with universal appeal. People are fascinated by watching wood being shaped on a lathe, because the effect is immediate and the shapes alter so quickly. A chunk of wood can be shaped with a chisel in a matter of minutes, whereas with other wood-oriented crafts, such as carving, progress is much slower. Even the final finish can be achieved on the lathe, either straight from the tool, by sanding, by burnishing with shavings or by applying wax as the work rotates. You can turn small functional objects, such as bowls and goblets, as well as make turned components for furniture, such as chair and table legs.

SEE ALSO
Measuring and marking, *pages 32–41*

Sawing, *pages 42–61*

Drilling and hammering, *pages 82–85*

Abrading, *pages 86–91*

Tool maintenance, *pages 92–99*

Finishes, *pages 174–181*

Woodturning lathe

The woodturning lathe is a quiet, relatively inexpensive machine that takes up little room. It consists of a motor that powers a variable-speed rotating spindle. The wood is precut into a more or less circular shape, mounted onto the lathe and spun at speed. A variety of differently profiled tools supported on a tool rest are fed against the revolving wood in order to cut different shapes.

⚠ Safety

Lathe work creates dust and chips that fly everywhere, so protect your eyes and lungs with an appropriate mask/face shield.

Motor housing
Fixed headstock
Drive spindle
Tailstock spindle
Sliding tailstock
Drive center
Tailstock center
Handwheel for moving tailstock
Adjustable tool rest
Lathe bed

Choice of lathe

The distance between the headstock and tailstock centers dictates the length of workpiece that you can turn; the depth of the lathe bed from the drive center determines the maximum diameter that can be turned. The wood is rotated in a holding device, such as a chuck; these come in various shapes and sizes to suit the type of work being undertaken. Bench lathes should be mounted to a sturdy workbench, so that the spindle centers are at or slightly above elbow height when your forearm is held in a relaxed position across the front of the body.

Choice of wood

Most woods lend themselves to turning. Some, such as pine, yew and elm, are especially suitable. Elm is often turned wet—that is, as unseasoned wood still containing a high degree of sap. Turning can make use of cutoffs that might be too small to use in other woodwork. A piece of wood prepared for turning on the lathe is called a blank.

Turning tools

Turning tools have sturdy handles and blades that are specially designed to withstand lathe work. Most blades are made of high-speed steel (HSS); HSS tools do not sharpen to quite as fine an edge as carbon-steel turning tools, but they hold that edge considerably longer. There are hundreds of turning tools available, but a basic set of six tools is fine for beginners.

▲ Roughing gouge

Use this square-tipped, U-shaped tool when spindle turning to rough out a blank from square section to round. Start about 2 in. (50mm) from the tailstock, and cut toward it. Repeat, starting each cut a little farther toward the headstock. When you reach about 2 in. (50mm) from the headstock, reverse the direction of the cut toward the headstock to complete the cylinder.

◀ Spindle gouge

Use this round-tipped gouge after the roughing gouge in spindle turning to cut coves, hollows, beads and a wide range of other shapes.

From left: Scraper, parting tool, oval skew chisel, standard skew chisel, spindle gouge, roughing gouge and bowl gouge.

Tool control

■ Hold the tool handle in one hand, in line with your forearm; use your other hand to control the blade, moving it from side to side along the tool rest.

■ For safety, it is vital that you support the tool on the tool rest before it touches the workpiece.

■ Try to develop a slicing action with the tool to achieve a smoother cut. First, rest the bevel on the wood, then lift the handle to engage the tip of the tool with the wood as you move the tool along the tool rest; angle the cutting edge in the direction you are moving.

■ When spindle turning, you should stand parallel to the lathe, a comfortable distance away, with your feet about shoulder-width apart, so that as you traverse the tool you can sway your body rather than move your feet. The tool handle should be beside your hip, not in front of your body.

▶ Skew chisel

This is a difficult tool to master, but one of the most versatile. Use it to do the job of a hand plane, producing a smooth, clean surface that needs little or no sanding, as well as to make a variety of cuts, such as a V-shaped groove. Skews come in two sections: oval and standard; the latter (shown here) is more suitable for beginners.

Smooth planing cut

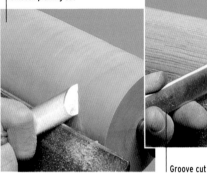

Groove cut

◀ Parting tool

In addition to its primary function, that of parting finished items from their waste blocks, you can use a parting tool to perform a variety of other tasks, such as to make sizing cuts in conjunction with calipers.

▶ Bowl gouge

Use this long, deep-fluted gouge for cutting the curves and hollows of bowls.

◀ Scraper

There are numerous shapes and styles of scraper; a multi-tip shear scraper is very versatile, and can be used on both crossgrain and end grain. When working crossgrain, scrapers should only be used to produce the best possible finish before sanding.

Sharpening tools

■ Turning tools are quickly blunted by the amount of wood that they remove, so they need to be sharpened more often than other hand tools. Whereas standard chisels and gouges have two bevel angles, turning tools only have a single bevel angle.

■ Make sure that you sharpen the whole face of the bevel on a gouge by rotating it slowly while maintaining the correct angle.

■ High-speed steel (HSS) tools are not affected by overheating; do not quench them when grinding, because HSS contracts very quickly, causing fine cracks that could fracture.

■ Scrapers need a burr to work; push a slipstone once or twice along the edge to raise a fine burr.

Spindle turning

Also known as turning between centers, spindle turning is done with the workpiece fixed between the drive center and tail center of the lathe, with the grain running parallel to the lathe's axis. One-center turning is done with the workpiece fixed to the drive center only, but still with the grain running parallel. Cutting is always made from the largest diameter to the smallest, cutting with the grain rather than against it. The best tool for spindle work is the skew chisel, although the gouge is easier to master.

Turning between centers

◀ **1** Cut a spindle blank, either square or octagonal; allow waste wood at each end for attaching to the centers. Mark the center of the wood at each end. There are all sorts of gadgets for this, but the simplest method is to draw diagonal lines. Where the lines intersect, make a small indentation with an awl. Use a mallet to attach the drive center to the center of the blank, then mount the drive center onto the headstock spindle.

▶ **2** Move the tailstock up to the other end of the wood, and use the handwheel to screw the tail center into it. Lathes can have two types of tail center. A live center rotates with the wood; a dead center is fixed. A little wax can be used on a dead center to prevent friction burn. Position the tool rest parallel to the wood, and about level with the centers. Rotate the wood manually to check that it clears the tool rest by at least ¼ in. (6mm).

◀ **3** Use a roughing gouge to turn the blank into a cylinder (see page 166). You can now shape and smooth the spindle, using a spindle gouge, skew chisel and parting tool, and apply a finish if required (see page 171). Use the parting tool to cut the work from the waste wood; support the piece as it comes free of the spindles.

One-center turning

▶ **1** After turning a cylinder between centers, you can mount the piece on a woodturning chuck to the drive center only, in the same way as when faceplate turning (see page 170). Position the tool rest at 90 degrees to the workpiece. Here, a hollow form is being shaped. Start by wrapping masking tape around a spindle gouge to set the depth of the hollow. Line up the point of the gouge with the center of the cylinder and plunge it in.

◀ **2** Start hollowing out the shape, making small cuts in an arc from the center outward. As you get deeper into the bowl, you may need to use a scraper, which has a stiffer shank. You can use a special cranked hollowing tool to hollow out bulbous forms with narrow necks where you cannot see inside the hollow.

▶ **3** Continue shaping the outside of the piece as necessary, just as you would when turning between centers.

Decorative spindle cuts

Spindles can be turned with a variety of decorative shapes. Mark the positions of the shapes in pencil first, by holding the pencil against the tool rest as the lathe turns. Use calipers to check that the sizes of the shapes are consistent.

- ■ **Beads:** Slide a skew chisel in a horizontal arc to form the curve of a bead.
- ■ **Hollows:** Sweep a spindle gouge from side to side to hollow out the spindle.
- ■ **Slots:** Drive a parting tool into the rotating work to create slotted features.

Hollow | Bead | Slot

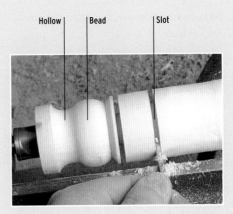

Faceplate turning

Faceplate turning is done with the grain running at 90 degrees to the lathe's axis; this means that you have two areas of end grain to deal with. The work is either screwed onto a faceplate or held in a woodturning chuck and mounted on the drive spindle. The spindle-turning rule of cutting from the largest diameter to the smallest applies less to faceplate turning; you have to think more of cutting with the grain, so that the fibers being cut are supported by the fibers beneath them.

Turning a bowl

▶ 1 Cut a circular or octagonal bowl blank and mount it onto the drive spindle. You can do this in several ways. A faceplate is a metal disk (supplied with most lathes) that provides a secure hold for larger pieces of crossgrain work. Position the faceplate over the center of the blank. Predrill screw holes, and then screw the faceplate to the blank. You can screw the faceplate to a disk of scrap hardwood glued to the center of the blank if you wish.

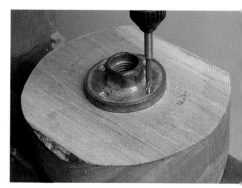

◀ 2 Alternatively, use a woodturning chuck mounted onto the drive spindle. There are different types of chuck; a combination chuck is ideal. When turning the outside of a bowl, drill a hole of the required depth in the center of the blank to match the screw of the chuck. Screw the blank firmly onto the chuck.

▶ 3 Create a foot or recess at the center of the blank; this will be used for mounting the bowl to hollow out the inside later. Set a pair of dividers to the diameter of the chuck jaws. Transfer this measurement to the bowl, being careful to let only one point of the dividers touch the wood.

4 Align the tool rest across the work, making sure that the wood can rotate freely. Use a bowl gouge to start cutting the recess (shown here) or foot; cut inside the scribed line for a recess, or outside for a foot. Use the long point of a skew chisel to cut a dovetailed edge for the chuck jaws to grip or expand into.

▶ **5** Use a roughing gouge to profile the outside of the bowl, working from the center outward. Adjust the position of the tool rest when necessary. Refine the curve with a bowl gouge and then scraper; when finished, sand smooth, working through the grits.

◀ **6** Clean out the foot or recess, and then mount it onto the chuck jaws.

▼ **7** Shape the inside of the bowl in the same way as the outside, working from the center outward. Finish as before.

Finishing on the lathe

■ **Sanding:** Sand pieces while they are still on the lathe. It is best to sand spindles by hand to retain crispness of detail. You can use a self-powered sander for bowls; this is basically a handle with a sanding pad at the end that is pressed against the rotating wood.

■ **Decoration:** You can create wonderful textural effects with a variety of tools, moving them against the rotating wood; take care with safety.

■ **Finishes:** A wax can be applied while the work is spinning, but it is best to rotate the wood by hand for lacquers or oils to avoid splashes.

5
Finishes and fittings

Advice on enhancing and protecting
projects with the right finishing touches

Choosing a finish

Most objects in wood require a coating of some kind, known as a finish, both to protect the wood and to enhance its appearance. Although you can use any type of finish on any type of wood, the choice will depend upon the nature of the piece and how and where it is to be used—for example, a hard lacquer finish may provide the best protection for a table surface, while the wood of a decorative item that needs less protection can be enhanced by an oil finish.

◀ ▼ Types of finish
1 Beeswax
2 Linseed oil
3 Tung or Danish oil
4 Nitrocellulose lacquer
5 Polyurethane varnish
6 Wood stain
7 Shellac flakes
8 Aerosol can of lacquer finish

Low, medium or high build

A finish can either be flat, satin or high gloss, and may have a low, medium or high build (thickness). The higher the gloss required, the more build of finish has to be applied. A high-build finish will also protect the wood more than a low-build one.

■ **Low-build finishes,** such as wax or oil, give minimal protection but allow the natural character of the wood to predominate. Dirt will easily get into the grain, and the pores and finish will need to be regularly attended to.

■ **A medium-build finish,** such as several coats of a fine oil or a microporous lacquer, seals the wood grain but does not completely encapsulate it. You can see and feel the grain through the finish.

■ **A high-build finish,** such as polyurethane varnish, fills the grain completely, which inhibits wood movement due to the loss or intake of moisture in the air. You can see the wood's color and pattern, but not feel its texture.

Finish	Appearance	Durability	Suitability
Wax: Beeswax is soft natural wax; a mix of beeswax and other waxes is easier to apply. Wax polish is usually a mixture of carnauba wax with beeswax or paraffin wax.	Soft shine that enhances the natural beauty of the wood.	Poor; needs regular attention if used alone. Wax polish is slightly more resilient than pure beeswax.	Generally best applied over another finish that seals the wood, such as lacquer. A wax-only finish can attract dirt, so avoid it on open-grained woods.
Oil: Oil finishes include linseed, teak, Danish and tung oils. Most wood finishing oils are based on tung oil, a natural oil that penetrates the wood. Linseed oil can also be mixed with an oil-based varnish.	Warm glow that enhances grain. Oil/varnish mixes can be applied as a high-build finish.	Fair; recoating may be necessary. An oil/varnish mix has greater durability.	Ideal for open-grained woods. Two or three coats will build up a soft sheen without obscuring the wood's tactile qualities.
Shellac: Shellac is a natural resin that can be bought as flakes that you mix with denatured alcohol, or ready-mixed. It is also a constituent of French polish.	Warm tint; beautifully lustrous when applied using French-polishing technique.	Moderate; will not withstand heat or moisture.	Makes an ideal sanding sealer before applying a wax finish. As a finish in itself, it can be low or high build (French polish).
Nitrocellulose lacquer: A fast-drying finish, available as gloss, satin or flat. Water-based lacquers are nonflammable, with less fumes than solvent-based ones.	Clear gloss; water-based versions have slightly poorer color.	Good; water-based lacquers are slightly less durable than solvent-based ones.	Items that receive moderate usage and where appearance is also important.
Polyurethane varnish: Easy-to-apply synthetic resin, available as gloss, satin or flat. It gives off terrible fumes when first applied. Less toxic versions include polyurethane gels and water-based acrylic varnishes. The latter are faster drying and nonflammable.	Clear; high-build finish can look plasticky; water-based versions can have a cold tinge.	Excellent; two-part varnishes are stronger than standard one-part varnishes. Gels and acrylics are not as resistant to water.	Items that receive heavy usage.

Preparing the surface

Before applying a finish, you must prepare the wood surfaces, because any imperfections will be made more apparent by the finish. Any holes should be filled and then sanded smooth, and all marks should be removed. Edges should be slightly softened by rounding them with sandpaper. You can also color the wood at this stage, using wood stain, bleach or ammonia.

SEE ALSO
Abrading,
pages 86–91

▶ Scraping and sanding

Use a scraper if necessary to remove any glue spots and level the surface. Then sand by hand or machine, working through the grits from coarse to fine—for example, use 100-, 180- and then 240-grit sandpaper. Remove the dust between sandings by wiping with a tack cloth. Use 240-grit paper for a final sanding by hand.

◀ Filling holes

There are all kinds of fillers on the market, in a range of colors and formulas. However, to be sure of a perfect color match, you can make a wood filler from sanded dust taken from the actual item, mixed with a drop of nitrocellulose lacquer. Work the filler into any knot holes using a fine putty knife, or a plastic or cardboard spatula. When dry, lightly sand with fine-grit sandpaper.

▶ Raising dents

If indentations in the surface are deep, it is best to raise them rather than try to sand them out or fill them. Dampen the surface around the dent with a cloth soaked in water. Fold the damp cloth and lay it over the dented area. Place the tip of a very hot iron onto the cloth and press gently. When dry, lightly sand with fine-grit paper.

▶ Staining

Wood stains are useful if you want to enrich the appearance of a wood that has an undistinguished color (for example, some of the mahoganies) or to use a non-wood color (primary colors, for instance). Most stains are oil- or water-based, the former being easier to apply and the latter deeper penetrating. Check the manufacturer's instructions to be sure that the stain you use is compatible with the final finish. Follow the manufacturer's instructions to apply the stain; when dry, denib the surface (see page 178).

◀ Bleaching

Bleaches are used to lighten the color of wood. You can use household bleach, but a special two-part wood bleach generates a stronger reaction. Always test the bleach on scrapwood first.

▶ Fuming

Ammonia fumes color wood that contains tannic acid; oak, for example, turns from golden to dark brown. You need to create a sealed environment, such as a tent of clear polythene, and make sure that all necessary surfaces are exposed.

Finishing sequence

1 Sand through the grits.

2 Fill any holes.

3 Final hand sanding.

4 If using a water-based finish, raise the grain and denib (see page 178).

5 Stain or color wood if required.

6 Fill grain if required.

7 Apply sealer (see page 178).

8 Apply finish (see pages 178–181).

◀ Filling the grain

If the wood is open-grained, such as oak or ash, the grain may need to be filled if you wish to achieve a smooth finish. Swab a generous amount of a color-matched filler onto the surface, and use a cloth to work it into the grain; an oil-bound filler is being applied here. Rub with a circular motion and wipe off the excess across the grain. A shellac sanding sealer can be used to fill and seal the grain at the same time (see page 178). Finally, sand the dry filler with fine-grit sandpaper.

Applying a finish

After the wood surfaces have been prepared, you can apply the finish in several ways. You can rub it on using a cloth or steel wool, apply it with a brush or use a spray gun. Most finishes require several coats, with the wood being lightly sanded (denibbed) between coats, and a final buffing with a soft cloth or steel wool at the end to produce a sheen. Follow the manufacturer's instructions for the particular finish you are using.

◀ Sealing the wood

Sealing is used to prevent the finish from being absorbed into the wood, as well as to prevent any wood stain from bleeding into the finish. The first coat of a finish usually acts as a sealer, but a special sealant is sometimes preferable, such as on very porous woods; check the manufacturer's recommendations for the finish you are using. Shellac sanding sealer is being applied here to seal the grain for a wax finish. Once the sealer is dry, denib the surface and wipe it with a tack cloth.

Wax

▶ 1 While not absolutely necessary, it is a good idea to seal the wood first. Then apply the wax in a very thin film with the finest grade of steel wool or a cloth. Use light pressure and a circular motion to work the wax into the grain.

◀ 2 Allow the wax to dry, then apply more coats if required. Finish by using a soft, dry cloth to buff the surface to a sheen.

Denibbing

If you wet a piece of wood, or seal it with a thin coat of varnish or shellac and let it dry, the grain will feather up to some extent, so that it feels hairy to the touch. Before you can achieve a super-smooth surface, these feathers or grain hairs need to be sanded off. The hairs are called nibs, and the procedure of sanding them off is called denibbing. In denibbing, you dampen the surface with water, let it dry and then sand the nibs off with the finest grit sandpaper.

Oil

▶ **1** You can apply oil with a paintbrush or cloth. Apply a liberal coating to the whole object and allow it to soak in; the time will vary according to the manufacturer's recommendations and the weather conditions. After the appropriate time, wipe off any excess oil with a paper towel.

▶ **2** For best results, allow the item to dry overnight, then lightly rub it with fine steel wool, to remove any dust particles that dried with the oil. Apply one or two more coats of oil in the same way. Finish by buffing to a sheen using fine steel wool and then a soft, dry cloth.

⚠ Safety

Never leave an oily cloth rolled up because it can combust spontaneously. Allow oily cloths to dry outdoors, unrolled, even if you simply intend to throw the cloth away afterward.

Shellac (French polishing)

◀ **1** Shellac can be applied with a brush, but the traditional technique of French polishing uses a pad. To make a polishing pad, wrap a ball of batting inside a linen cloth.

▼ **3** For a high-gloss finish, use the pad to work over the surface with denatured alcohol. For a satin or flat finish, buff with fine-grade steel wool and wax, or a brush and very fine-grade pumice powder.

▶ **2** Apply several coats, using a little polish and a fast circular motion; allow half an hour or so between coats. French polish is also known as white polish, button polish or garnet polish, depending on the color of the polish.

High gloss   Satin

Polyurethane varnish

▶ **1** Polyurethane gels are very easy to apply with a cloth, but most polyurethane varnishes are applied with a brush. To obtain a deeper penetration, thin the first coat with about 10 percent mineral spirits.

◀ **2** Brush a liberal coating of varnish quickly and evenly along the grain, then allow to dry. Generally, two to three coats are desirable; denib the surface between coats (see page 178). Buff with a cloth to the sheen you require.

Nitrocellulose lacquer

◀ **1** Lacquer can be applied with a brush, pad or spray. Spraying gives a perfectly even finish. Practice on scrapwood first, adjusting the gun's rate of delivery as necessary. Move the gun in smooth sweeps, keeping the spray parallel to the surface. Overlap each stroke by 50 percent and spray past the ends of the piece. Apply subsequent coats in the same way, denibbing between them (see page 178).

⚠ Spraying safety

■ Most finishing materials are flammable and potentially explosive when sprayed. There must be no naked flames or lights. Do not smoke. An exhaust fan is necessary to remove fumes and overspray, as is some form of nonflammable curtaining or partition to separate the space. If much spraying has to be done, you will probably need to invest in a special spray booth.

■ The fumes given off by spraying can be harmful, and you will need some form of mask. The simplest is a dust mask, but for some finishes, a vapor mask may be necessary. With a lot of spraying, you may need a mask or helmet with an independent air supply.

▶ **2** Standing the work on a rotating platform allows you to spray all sides easily. When the lacquer has hardened, denib and wipe free from dust. After the final layer, apply a wax coating for a satin finish, or buff to a high-gloss finish.

▼ ▶ Decorative effects

Decorating wood with special effects is a craft that has developed with the demands of the market. Numerous different effects are possible, ranging from simple liming and spattering to more complex gilding and marbling.

Brushes

■ Standard paintbrushes, made from hog or horse hair, are used to apply stains, paints and varnishes. Buy good-quality brushes to achieve the best results. Some decorative effects require the use of special brushes, such as a badger-hair softening brush for applying a marbled finish.

■ The professional way to clean brushes is to suspend them in a cleaning solution so that the paint can drop off the end of the bristles without bending them out of line. Drill a small hole through the handle of the brush and thread a piece of sturdy wire or a nail through it. You can suspend several brushes from the same wire. Refer to the manufacturer's recommendations for the appropriate cleaning solution for the finish you are using.

1 Gilding
2 Crackle glaze
3 Marbling
4 Painted "wood grain"
5 Sprayed paint spatter
6 Liming

Hinges and locks

A wide choice of hardware is available to the woodworker. Visual appeal, strength, durability, size and function are important factors to consider when choosing the right hinge or lock. Most work needs good-quality hinges, the best being solid brass butt hinges. The technique illustrated here shows the procedure for attaching butt hinges to a box, but the same principles apply to hanging doors.

SEE ALSO

Holding and clamping, *pages 24–25*

Measuring and marking, *pages 32–41*

Sawing, *pages 42–61*

Planing, *pages 62–71*

Chiseling, *pages 72–75*

Drilling and hammering, *pages 82–85*

Abrading, *pages 86–91*

Inserting hinges

◀ **1** Mount the box firmly on the workbench. Decide where to place the two hinges; position each hinge a distance equal to its own length from opposite ends of the box. For larger items, you may need more hinges. Using a marking knife and the hinge itself as a template, mark the length of the hinge on the wood. Make sure that the center of the hinge pivot is exactly at the outer edge.

▶ **2** Using a try square, lightly square the lines across the wood to the approximate hinge width and down the edge to the approximate hinge thickness.

▼ **4** Gauge the width of each hinge recess. Reset the gauge to mark the depth of the hinge recess (again, the pin of the gauge should be set to the center of the hinge pivot) and repeat the process. Shade in the waste. Mark the hinges on the lid in the same way.

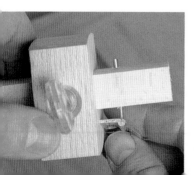

◀ **3** Set a marking gauge to width using the hinge itself. The pin of the gauge should be set to the center of the hinge pivot.

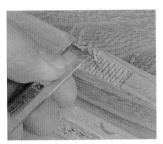

◀ 5 Using a chisel, carefully sever the waste fibers across the grain with a series of fine parallel cuts. Work from the center and move outward in each direction, carefully locating the chisel for each cut. Work the chisel horizontally to lift out the severed fibers to the required depth for the recess. Trim the ends of the recess across the grain to the line.

▶ 6 Insert a hinge and mark the center hole with a pencil. Using a drill or awl, make a pilot hole fractionally nearer the shoulder (where the long edge of the hinge will butt against) to ensure a tight fit when screwed in.

▼ 7 Run a finely set plane along the hinged edges of the box and lid to produce a slight bevel. This will allow the lid to swing freely.

◀ 8 Screw the hinges in position. In tough woods, insert a steel screw first to widen the pilot hole. Brass screws are much softer and are likely to break when driven into hard woods.

▼ 9 Drill the pilot holes for the remaining screws and insert them. It looks much neater if all the slots are in line or on the same diagonal.

◀ 10 When the box closes, the faces should meet with no more than the clearance of a thin piece of paper to allow for the thickness of the finish. Note that the hinge pivots protrude slightly. Any fractional misalignment can be sanded down with a sanding block.

Inserting a mortise lock

◄ **1** Place the lock on the edge of the wood to mark its overall outline (note that the lock is upside-down to do this). Use a try square and marking knife to mark the depth of the lock on the inside of the box.

▼ **3** Chisel out the waste horizontally across the grain, adjusting the depth of cut to match the shape of the recessed parts of the lock. In such a confined space, the trickiest part is to cut an accurate line along the grain at the bottom of the lock. Here, the bevel of the chisel is used to give a vertical cut.

► **2** Mark the depth of the various recessed features of the lock by holding it against the wood.

◄ **4** Mark the keyhole position using a marking gauge and try square to transfer the information from the lock.

Handles

There is a vast array of handles available. Your choice should be based on how the handles will look on the finished piece, as well as how well they will function.

◄ **5** Drill a slightly oversized hole for the keyhole. Using a coping saw, insert the blade into the hole, then carefully cut the keyhole verticals; trim with a narrow chisel.

◀ **6** Insert the lock into its recess and check that everything is level. In this confined space, use a nail with its tip flattened to hammer a pilot hole for the screw. Attach the lock with fine screws, and check that the key operates in the lock.

▶ **7** The catch plate has to be accurately recessed into the lid so that the key operates smoothly; it should sit level with the wood in the lid. Mark its profile with a try square and marking gauge.

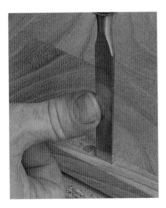

◀ **8** Recess the catch using the same methods as for recessing the hinges.

▶ **9** Drill pilot holes and attach the catch with fine screws, making sure that everything is perfectly level.

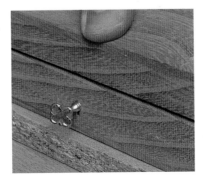

Stays

There are all kinds of lid and door stays available to prevent doors from opening too far and to support drop-down lids in the open position. They should come with instructions, but it may be worth doing a trial run with scrapwood first.

◀ **10** Plane a fine bevel along the edge as a continuation of the hinge bevel for visual effect.

6
Practical applications

Simple projects to put your woodworking
tools and techniques into practice

Small table

This small table is a classic, timeless design, and the techniques and processes used in making it can be applied to many other designs that use a frame construction. The table is a good first project for a beginner, providing a practical foundation in basic techniques and processes. If you are a beginner, choose a hardwood, because it is easier to achieve crisp saw and chisel cuts than with a softwood. A wood with a straight, close grain will also be easier to work. Select a color that will relate to the place where the table will be used.

Tool list

- Bar clamps
- Pencil; steel rule; marking knife; try square; marking gauge; mortise gauge
- Panel saw; tenon or dovetail saw
- Jack or smoothing plane
- Power router, or rabbet plane or shoulder plane
- Mortise chisel
- Nail set; drill and drill bits; screwdriver
- Cabinet scraper; sandpaper and sanding block

Cutting list

No.	Sawn	Planed
4 legs	22 x 1½ x 1½ in. (560 x 40 x 40mm)	19 x 1¼ x 1¼ in. (480 x 30 x 30mm)
4 upper rails	12 x 2 x 1 in. (305 x 50 x 25mm)	9½ x 1¾ x ¾ in. (240 x 45 x 20mm)
4 lower rails	12 x 1½ x 1 in. (305 x 40 x 25mm)	9½ x 1¼ x ¾ in. (240 x 30 x 20mm)
4 top frame sides	16 x 3¼ x 1 in. (406 x 80 x 25mm)	14 x 3 x ¾ in. (350 x 75 x 20mm)

Plus: Sheet material for inset top measuring 9 x 9 x ¼ in. (230 x 230 x 6mm); masking tape; glue; dowels; screws; finishing materials.

Note: Two thicknesses of board are needed: 1½ in. (40mm) and 1 in. (25mm). Buy one of each from which to cut the components. The rail length of 9½ in. (240mm) allows 8 in. (200mm) between shoulders, plus ¾ in. (20mm) each end for tenons.

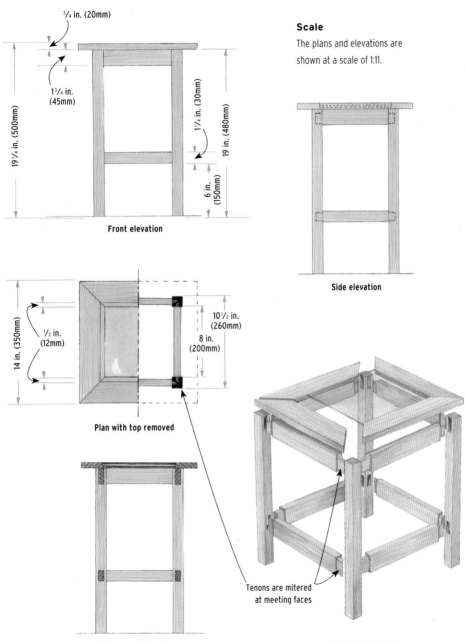

¾ in. (20mm)

1¾ in. (45mm)

1¼ in. (30mm)

19¼ in. (500mm)

19 in. (480mm)

6 in. (150mm)

Front elevation

Scale

The plans and elevations are shown at a scale of 1:11.

Side elevation

14 in. (350mm)

½ in. (12mm)

10½ in. (260mm)

8 in. (200mm)

Plan with top removed

Sectional end elevation

Tenons are mitered at meeting faces

Exploded diagram

Making the table

◄ **1** Mark and cut all the components, and plane them square; leave the legs overlong to make cutting the joints easier. Clamp the legs together and use a pencil to mark the length of the legs, the positions of the rails and the length of the mortises. The mortises for the lower rails should allow for tenons with a shoulder all around; the mortises for the upper rails should allow for a sloping haunch at the top. Pencil in the mortise waste.

SEE ALSO
Holding and clamping,
pages 24—25
Core tools and techniques,
pages 28—99
Gluing and clamping,
pages 106—107
Dowel joints,
pages 116—117
Mortise-and-tenon joints,
pages 126—131
Veneering,
pages 148—153
Finishes,
pages 172—181

▲ **2** Unclamp the legs. Using a try square, transfer all the pencil marks from the face side to the face edge. Use a marking knife to scribe cut lines at each end of the mortises, and all around the top and bottom of the legs (the legs will be trimmed to length later). Use a mortise gauge to scribe the sides of the mortises. This will give you four legs, with joints marked on the eight inside faces.

▶ **3** Clamp the four upper rails together and mark the overall rail length of 8 in. (200mm), plus ³/₄ in. (20mm) at each end for the tenons. Repeat this procedure with the lower rails clamped together, using one of the upper rails as a measuring stick to make sure that both sets of rails are exactly the same. Transfer the marks to the other three faces of each rail, then cut them to length.

▶ **4** Use the mortise gauge to mark the tenons around the edges and end of each rail. Use a marking gauge to mark the edge shoulders and haunches on the sides of each rail; square these marks across the edges. Pencil in the waste that is to be cut away.

◀ **5** There are 16 stopped mortises to cut in the legs; each mortise should be ¾ in. (20mm) deep. Clamp the work in a vise and chisel out the waste up to the scribed lines.

▼ **7** Chisel out the waste to accept the haunched tenon.

▶ **6** In the eight mortises for the top rails, make the entry for the haunch by sawing the ends of the mortise at an angle.

▼ **9** Cut the sloping line of the haunch.

▼ **10** Lay each piece flat to cut the main tenon shoulder.

▲ **8** There are eight tenons with haunch and edge shoulders, and eight with two edge shoulders. Saw down to the shoulders on all tenon pieces in the same way.

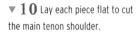

▶ **11** Mark two drill holes in the underside of each upper rail for the screws to hold the top frame. To avoid having to use very long screws, drill a hole slightly larger than the screw head to a predetermined depth, then drill a clearance hole all the way through for the screw. The screw then sits in the hole, allowing a shorter screw to be used.

◀ **12** Number or letter each joint and carefully fit each tenon into its mortise. Note that the tenons at each corner will meet; cut a miter on the end of each one so that they fit in the mortise together. Check and recheck that you have marked this correctly before you cut; adjust as necessary to achieve an accurate fit.

▶ **13** Check that the frame is flat and square, and that the diagonals are identical. If all is well, apply glue and clamp together. Wipe away any excess glue.

◀ **14** Repeat this process to assemble the whole underframe of the table. Always do a dry run first, before applying glue. When dry, remove the clamps and saw off the waste at the top and bottom of the legs; plane the end grain flat.

15 On each of the four pieces for the top frame, cut a ¼-in. (6mm) deep rabbet along the inner edge. Mark miters at the corners and saw accurately to this line. Glue triangular pieces of scrapwood to the outside corners to aid assembly. Plane the miters so that all faces fit.

16 Use a marking gauge to scribe a center line along each mitered edge. Carefully align the four frame pieces in the vise, with mitered edges uppermost. Square three lines across the pieces; the intersection between these lines and the gauged center lines on each piece indicates the centers of the dowel holes. Use a hammer and nail set to mark location points for the bit, then drill the holes for the dowels.

17 Assemble the mitered dowel joints dry and make any necessary adjustments; the scrapwood triangles allow you to apply clamping pressure at right angles to the joint face. When the joints fit correctly, apply glue and clamp together. When the glue has dried, remove the clamps and chisel or saw off the triangular blocks.

18 Plane all outside surfaces, then screw the underframe to the top frame. Scrape and sand the table, and apply a finish. Double-check the dimensions of the recess and insert the top of your choice. Here, a piece of plywood has been embellished with four diamond-matched squares of veneer.

Nursery furniture

This nursery furniture is an ideal opportunity to explore the possibilities of working with manmade board. The construction is straightforward, and the joints can be reinforced with biscuits or splines. The decorative possibilities are limited only by your imagination.

The prototype has been spray painted in primary colors, with decorative "falling letters." MDF was used because it is so simple to finish, but plywood or chipboard would work equally well.

Tool list

- Bar clamps; C clamps
- Pencil; steel rule; marking knife; try square; marking gauge
- Coping saw, jigsaw or bandsaw
- Jack or smoothing plane
- Power router or biscuit jointer
- Sandpaper and sanding block

Cutting list

Boards: Two thicknesses of board are required: $3/8$ in. (10mm) for the table and main chair frame, and $1/8$ in. (3mm) or $3/16$ in. (4.5mm) for the chair seat and back. To reduce waste, refer to the layout diagrams on pages 196 and 198 to help you calcuate overall dimensions required.

Plus: Masking tape; biscuits, or plywood for splines; glue; finishing materials.

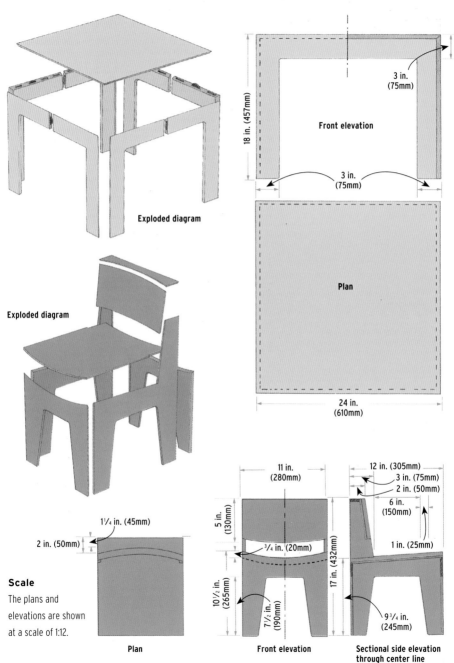

Exploded diagram

3 in. (75mm)

Front elevation

3 in. (75mm)

18 in. (457mm)

Plan

24 in. (610mm)

Exploded diagram

1¼ in. (45mm)

2 in. (50mm)

Scale

The plans and elevations are shown at a scale of 1:12.

11 in. (280mm)

12 in. (305mm)

3 in. (75mm)

2 in. (50mm)

6 in. (150mm)

5 in. (130mm)

¾ in. (20mm)

17 in. (432mm)

1 in. (25mm)

10½ in. (265mm)

7½ in. (190mm)

9¾ in. (245mm)

Plan

Front elevation

Sectional side elevation through center line

Making the table

▶ **1** Follow the diagram to lay out the components on the board, with the L-shaped legs grouped around the tabletop. This utilizes the material as economically as possible. Use a coping saw, jigsaw or bandsaw to cut the components. Sand any rough edges.

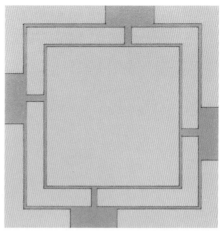

◀ **2** Plane a 45-degree miter around the outer edges of each leg component, and all around the tabletop.

▶ **3** Rout grooves for splines along all the mitered edges. Rout another groove where the leg components will meet to form a rail under the tabletop. Cut splines from a piece of plywood of the same thickness as the grooves. Alternatively, use a biscuit jointer to make short grooves for biscuits.

Tabletop joint options

The eight L-shaped legs are mitered together in pairs to form four leg-and-rail corner components. To fit these to the top, you can either miter the tabletop and the tops of the corner components, or set the legs directly under the top. The project is described using miters all around.

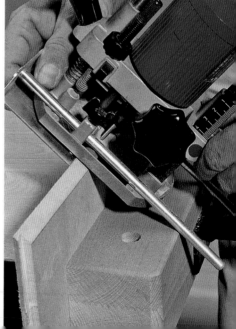

▲ **4** Assemble the four corner joints using two L-shaped pieces per corner. Note that the long sections form the legs, and the short sections fit to the tabletop. Use masking tape to hold the joints together. Make sure that the corners are square and allow to dry.

SEE ALSO

Holding and clamping, *pages 24–25*

Core tools and techniques, *pages 28–99*

Gluing and clamping, *pages 106–107*

Splined edge joint, *page 114*

Biscuit joints, *pages 118–119*

Shaping and bending, *pages 140–147*

Finishes, *pages 172–181*

◄ **5** Glue two leg assemblies to the tabletop on opposite corners, then fit the final pair of legs. Not only will you be spline- or biscuit-jointing the legs to the top, but you will also be jointing the rail between each leg section.

▶ **6** Plane or sand off all sharp edges and corners, or use a router with a round-over bit. Sand the table all over, and then apply a sealing coat. MDF needs slightly less sealing than either chipboard or plywood, but all types of manmade board require sealing before applying a finish. Sand lightly between each coat. Apply the finish and any decorative effects you wish.

Making the chair

▶ **7** Follow the diagram to lay out the components on the board; if you are making more than one chair, you will probably be able to use the material more economically. You may need to cut the seat and back slightly oversize (see step 11). Using a coping saw, jigsaw or bandsaw, cut the components. Plane to the required shape, paying attention to the sloping angle on the inside edges of the legs and back.

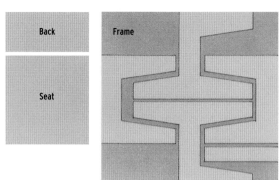

Back

Seat

Frame

◀ **8** Cut miters on the four corners of the main sections where they will be joined to form the legs. Take care to stop the miter on the back leg above the seat position. Cut miters where the top rail fits to the back.

▶ **9** Cut rabbets to accommodate the seat and back rest. Prepare spline-and-groove or biscuit joints, as you did for the table.

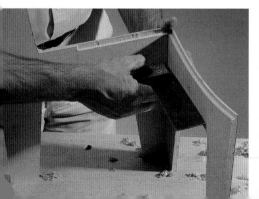

◀ **10** Assemble the frame dry, including the top rail, and make any necessary adjustments. If all is well, glue and allow to dry.

▶ **11** If you have used thin material for the seat and back, it will bend to the curve easily. If not, cut them very slightly oversize, and clamp them in a form to bend them. Here, three boards are used as a simple but effective form.

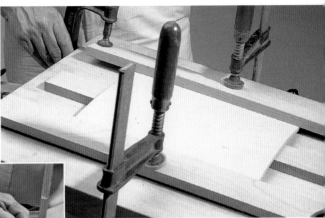

◀ **12** Fit the seat in the rabbets, marking where it needs to be cut away to fit inside the side frames at the back. This is a tricky piece of measuring, so take care.

▶ **13** When the seat fits, glue and clamp in position. The same, but slightly easier procedure, applies for the back rest. Fit and glue in position.

◀ **14** Sand off all sharp edges or use a router with a round-over bit. Finish the chair in the same way as the table. Use filler if necessary, sand all over, apply sealing coats, the finishing coat and any decorative design you wish.

Chest of drawers

This project consists of a basic cabinet containing four drawers, each of a different depth. The drawers are opened by finger grooves positioned so that they form a distinctive design feature across the cabinet front. Classic fine furniture-making techniques used in this chest of drawers include dovetail drawer joints, and dust boards between the drawers. If this is your first time making drawers, choose a wood that is fairly easy to work. Beech is useful for the drawer sides and interior parts of the cabinet, while the drawer fronts and outside of the cabinet can be any wood of your choice.

Tool list

- Bar clamps
- Pencil; steel rule; marking knife; try square; marking gauge; mortise gauge
- Panel saw; dovetail saw
- Jack or smoothing plane
- Range of bevel-edged chisels for dovetails; mortise chisel
- Power router; biscuit jointer or drill (depending on your choice of corner joints)
- Cabinet scraper; sandpaper and sanding block

Cutting list: Cabinet

No.	Sawn	Planed
2 sides	27 x 13½ x 1¼ in. (686 x 343 x 30mm)	26 x 13 x 1 in. (660 x 330 x 25mm)
1 top	17 x 13½ x 1¼ in. (432 x 343 x 30mm)	16 x 13 x 1 in. (406 x 330 x 25mm)
1 bottom rail	17 x 3 x 1 in. (432 x 75 x 25mm)	16 x 2⅞ x ¾ in. (406 x 72 x 20mm)
8 drawer cross rails	16 x 2¼ x ¾ in. (406 x 57 x 20mm)	2 x ½ in. (50 x 12mm)
8 drawer runners	8 x 1½ x ¾ in. (200 x 38 x 20mm)	1¼ x ½ in. (30 x 12mm)
1 cabinet back	14 x 16 x ¼ in. (660 x 406 x 6mm) plywood	
4 dust boards	13 x 8 x ¼ in. (330 x 200 x 6mm) plywood	

Plus: Glue; screws; finishing materials.

Exploded diagram

Joints at junction of top and sides can be mitered and reinforced with splines, biscuits or dowels (ideal for a beginner), or jointed with a more complex blind mitered dovetail

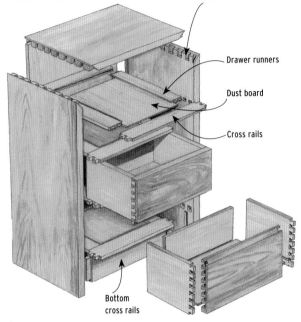

Drawer runners

Dust board

Cross rails

Bottom cross rails

SEE ALSO

Holding and clamping, *pages 24–25*

Core tools and techniques, *pages 28–99*

Gluing and clamping, *pages 106–107*

Splined edge joint, *page 114*

Dowel joints, *pages 116–117*

Biscuit joints, *pages 118–119*

Mortise-and-tenon joints, *pages 126–131*

Dovetail joints, *pages 132–137*

Finishes, *pages 172–181*

Cutting list: Drawers

No.		1st (top) drawer	2nd	3rd	4th
1 front	Sawn	15 x 4¼ x 1 in. (380 x 105 x 25mm)	5½ in. (140mm)	6½ in. (162mm)	7½ in. (190mm)
	Planed	14 x 4 x ¾ in. (356 x 100 x 20mm)	5 in. (130mm)	6 in. (150mm)	7 in. (180mm)
2 sides	Sawn	12 x 3¾ x ¾ in. (305 x 90 x 20mm)	4¾ in. (120mm)	5¾ in. (146mm)	6¾ in. (172mm)
	Planed	11 x 3½ x ½ in. (280 x 85 x 12mm)	4½ in. (115mm)	5½ in. (140mm)	6½ in. (162mm)
1 back	Sawn	15 x 3 x ¾ in. (380 x 75 x 20mm)	4 in. (100mm)	5 in. (130mm)	6 in. (150mm)
	Planed	14 x 2⅞ x ⅜ in. (356 x 72 x 10mm)	3⅞ in. (95mm)	4⅞ in. (122mm)	5⅞ in. (148mm)
1 bottom		14 x 11 x ¼ in. (356 x 280 x 6mm) plywood			

Note: All of the drawers are the same length and thickness, but the drawer depth changes, with the deepest drawer at the bottom of the chest. The width of board therefore changes for each drawer. In the above list, all three dimensions are listed for the top drawer; only the width of board is specified for the other three drawers, because the other dimensions remain the same.

Scale

The plans and elevations are shown at a scale of 1:8 unless indicated otherwise.

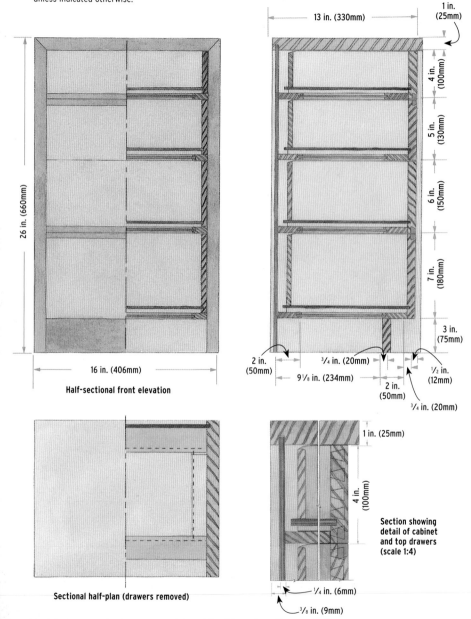

Sectional side elevation through center line

13 in. (330mm)

1 in. (25mm)

4 in. (100mm)

5 in. (130mm)

6 in. (150mm)

7 in. (180mm)

3 in. (75mm)

26 in. (660mm)

16 in. (406mm)

Half-sectional front elevation

2 in. (50mm)

³/₄ in. (20mm)

9 ¹/₈ in. (234mm)

¹/₂ in. (12mm)

2 in. (50mm)

³/₄ in. (20mm)

1 in. (25mm)

4 in. (100mm)

Section showing detail of cabinet and top drawers (scale 1:4)

Sectional half-plan (drawers removed)

¹/₄ in. (6mm)

³/₈ in. (9mm)

Making the chest

▶ **1** Mark and cut all the components, and plane them square; leave everything slightly over length. Mark the positions of all the cross rails on the two sides. Mark and then rout the grooves on the sides and top to accommodate the back panel.

◀ **2** Make the top corner joints. The easiest method is to miter them, and add splines, biscuits or dowels for reinforcement.

▶ **3** Alternatively, use blind mitered dovetail joints. Mark the shoulders on the inside faces; mark the miter on the edges. Cut a rabbet across the end, about two-thirds the thickness of the wood. Mark the pins on the top piece.

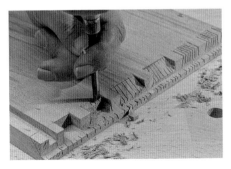

◀ **4** Cut the pins and remove the waste by a series of saw cuts and by paring with a chisel.

▶ **5** Working on one joint at a time, mark the tails on the side pieces, using the cut pins as a template. Remove the waste. Cut the miter on the edges and along the end lip. You should then be able to tap the dovetail together.

◀ **6** Mark the bottom cross rail with a tenon at each end with shoulders all around; make stopped mortises on the two sides to accommodate the tenons. Slide the back section into place from the bottom. Sand the interior, and apply an interior finish if required.

▶ **7** Under each drawer is a frame consisting of a runner on each side and a front and back cross rail. The cross rails are tenoned into stopped mortises in the cabinet, and the runners are tenoned into a groove in the cross rails. A plywood dust board is set within grooves cut on the inside edges of these pieces. The runners and dust boards are slightly undersize from front to back. Mark out the components.

▼ **8** Make twin tenons at each end of the back and front cross rails, and make corresponding stopped mortises on the inside of the cabinet. Cut the groove on the inside edge of the cross rails, and a tenon at each end of the runners.

Drawer runners

The design assumes that the sides are made from solid wood; therefore, there is likely to be wood movement. To allow for expansion and contraction, the tenon on the drawer runners should be fitted tight and glued at the front, while at the back the tenon and its shoulder should be cut short by about $1/8$ in. (3mm) to allow for any back-to-front movement in the cabinet.

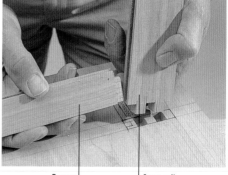

Runner | Cross rail

► **9** Fit the carcass together dry. Make any adjustments, then take it apart again.

◄ **10** Mark the positions of the front-to-back drawer runners on the inside of the sides. Remember that these are tenoned not into a mortise, but into the groove in the cross rails. Cut a groove for the dust board in each runner. Mark, cut and fit four plywood dust boards.

► **11** Try assembling all the components together. If all is well, make sure that all the internal sections are sanded and then glue and clamp the carcass together. It is not usual to apply a finish to the inside of drawers, but you can apply a simple sealing coat of the chosen finish if you wish. Drawers should slide wood onto wood. You should now have a firm carcass structure in which to run the drawers.

◄ **12** Make and fit the first drawer. Start by planing the drawer sides so that they are an exact fit and will slide in and out of the carcass.

► **13** Each drawer back is not a tight fit vertically, because it sits on the drawer bottom and does not extend the full depth of the drawer. It does, however, need to fit precisely across the carcass and you should be able to insert it from front to back.

◄ **14** Fit the drawer front into its opening. It should fit from the underside of the cabinet top to the lower face of the first drawer rail. It should fit exactly on the inside face from end to end, but make a bevel so that it tapers toward the outside face, which is slightly longer. Make the groove for the drawer bottom on the inside of the two sides and the front.

Length of tails equals two-thirds thickness of front piece to allow for lapped section

Lapped section

► **15** Half-blind dovetails join the front to the sides, with the tails on the side pieces. This hides the mechanics of the joint on the front of the drawer. Set the marking gauge to the thickness of the wood and scribe the shoulder line for the pins on the inside of the front piece. Reset the gauge to two-thirds the thickness; scribe along the end grain and edges to indicate the lapped section. Use this gauge setting to scribe the shoulder lines of the tails on the side piece. Mark and cut the tails, and then the matching pins. Remember to make allowances for the handle groove that is on the lower edge of the top drawer. Mark and cut this groove.

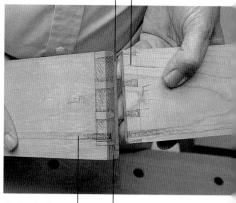

Marking for drawer-bottom groove

Marking for handle groove

▶ **16** Through dovetails join the sides to the back. Mark and cut the dovetails with care, making sure that your gauge lines are precisely the thickness of the components—this technique does not allow for major planing on the drawer sides to ensure fit.

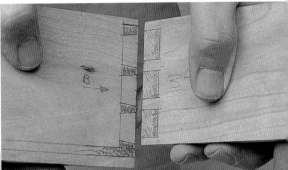

◀ **17** Mark the plywood bottom and cut to fit. Slide the bottom into place. The drawer bottom is not glued in the grooves; slot it in place and insert two screws at the back, through the drawer bottom and up into the drawer back. Assemble the drawer dry and check that it is a tight fit.

▶ **18** Add glue and assemble the drawer. When the glue has cured, it should only need a few touches of the plane to allow the drawer to run smoothly in its space. Follow the same procedure to make the remaining three drawers. Note that the handle groove is on the upper edge of the second drawer, the lower edge of the third drawer, and the upper edge of the bottom drawer. Attach the cabinet back with a couple of screws through the back into the bottom back drawer rail. Sand the carcass and drawer fronts, and apply the final finish.

Easy chair

This chair calls for two different shaping and bending techniques—shaping curved rails from solid wood, and making curved slats from laminated strips of veneer. Choose a sturdy looking wood, such as oak, ash, teak, beech or elm. The prototype was made in cherry. Your choice will be affected by the veneer available to you for the laminated back slats. The chair is comfortable as it is, but you could add a seat cushion made of leather or fabric filled with feathers.

Tool list

- Bar clamps; C clamps
- Pencil; steel rule at least 24 in. (610mm) long; marking knife; try square; marking gauge; mortise gauge
- Panel saw; dovetail saw; frame saw, jigsaw or bandsaw
- Jack or smoothing plane; spokeshave
- Power router, or rabbet plane or shoulder plane and hand router
- Range of chisels
- Drill and drill bits; screwdriver
- Cabinet scraper; rasps; files; sandpaper and sanding block

Cutting list

No.	Sawn	Planed
2 back legs	33 x 2 x 2 in. (838 x 50 x 50mm)	31 x 1³/₄ x 1³/₄ in. (787 x 45 x 45mm)
2 front legs	22 x 2 x 2 in. (560 x 50 x 50mm)	20 x 1³/₄ x 1³/₄ in. (508 x 45 x 45mm)
3 curved cross rails	24 x 3 full x 2¹/₂ in. (610 x 75 x 60mm)	22¹/₂ x 3 x 1¹/₄ in. (572 x 75 x 30mm) on curve
2 side rails and 2 arms	27 x 3 full x 1¹/₄ in. (686 x 75 x 30mm)	26 x 3 x 1 in. (660 x 75 x 25mm)
7 seat slats	21 x 2¹/₄ x ³/₄ in. (533 x 57 x 20mm)	20¹/₂ x 2 x ⁵/₈ in. (521 x 50 x 14mm)
6 back slats	30 x 2 x ¹/₂ in. (762 x 50 x 12mm) Each slat to be laminated from eight ¹/₁₆-in. (1.5mm) thick veneers	

Plus: About 30 x 6 x 2¹/₂ in. (762 x 50 x 1.5mm) joinery softwood to make the lamination form; large sheet of paper, or graph paper, for full-size drawing of back slats; plastic sheets; glue; screws; finishing materials.

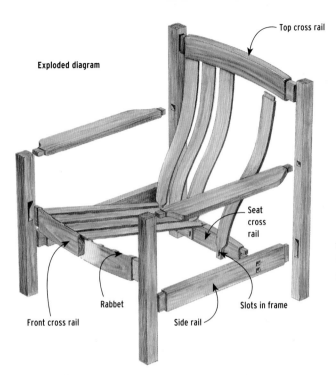

Exploded diagram

Top cross rail

Seat cross rail

Slots in frame

Side rail

Rabbet

Front cross rail

Back slat template

Each square on the template equals
1 in. (25mm). To make the form for
bending the laminated back slats,
enlarge the template to full size.
Do this with graph paper, or by making
a grid of squares and plotting the
points where the lines of the curve
cross. Transfer the whole shape onto
the center of a piece of softwood,
including marks to indicate the top
and bottom of the slat, plus the tenon.
Cut the shape and clean up the faces.

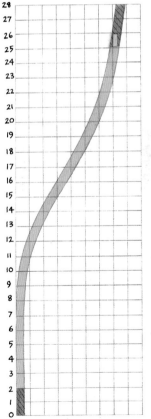

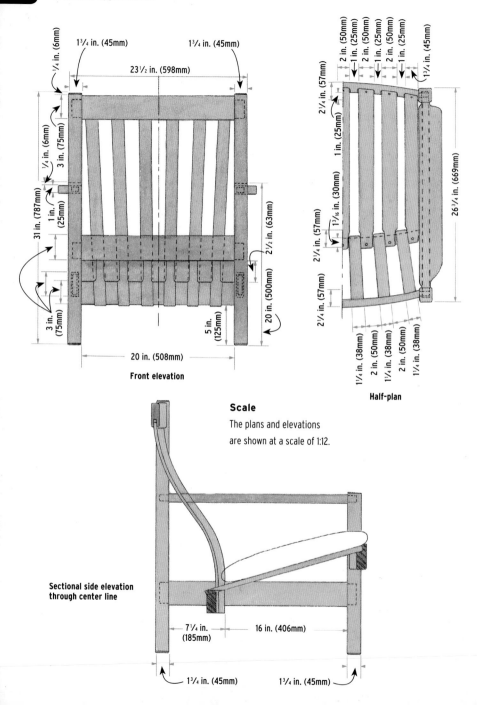

Front elevation

Half-plan

Scale

The plans and elevations
are shown at a scale of 1:12.

**Sectional side elevation
through center line**

Making the chair

▶ 1 Mark and cut all the components except the back slats, and plane them square; leave the legs slightly over length, and the cross rails slightly over thick. To make the side frames, mark the lengths of the legs and the positions of the stopped mortises for the side rails, arms and cross rails. Mark the tenons, with shoulders all around, at each end of the side rails and arms. Mark through mortises on the side rails to accommodate the twin through tenons on the seat cross rail; the seat cross rail should be set low in the side rail.

◀ 2 Double-check the marking, then scribe lines where you intend to cut. Cut the mortise-and-tenon joints for the two side frames, and the mortises for the cross rails. When cutting through mortises, remember to mark and cut from both sides.

▶ 3 Each arm is set so that the inside face is in line with the inside surfaces of the legs, and the outside edge protrudes. To shape the ends, drill a hole to make the inner curve and then saw into the hole. Finish the shaping with rasps, files and sandpaper.

◀ 4 Assemble both side frames dry, and make any necessary adjustments. Glue and clamp, wiping off any excess glue.

▶ **5** The three cross rails were prepared slightly over thick to allow for cutting the curves. Mark the length of the rail and tenons on each piece. Draw the curves with a pencil by bending a steel rule between the two end points and the center mark. It helps to have a partner to hold the ruler on the center mark and draw the line.

◀ **6** Trim the ends of all three rails to the overall rail thickness and pencil mark the tenons.

▶ **7** Saw the curves. Each rail has a planed surface top and bottom, square ends marked ready for the tenons, and a sawn curve on the outside and inside faces. Clean up the outside curve with a plane, except the ends near the tenons, which should be pared with a chisel. Smooth the inside curve with a spokeshave.

◀ **8** Mark and cut the tenons at each end of the top and front cross rails. Mark and cut the mortises on the underside of the top cross rail to accept the six back slats. Mark and cut twin through tenons at each end of the seat cross rail. The underside of this rail sits partly below the side rail, so the tenons should be made near the top of the seat cross rail to allow for this.

▶ **9** Number or letter all of the joints, then assemble the whole frame dry. The front cross rail needs a bevel at the top edge for the seat slats to lie flat, so place a steel rule between the seat and front cross rails to measure how much bevel is needed. Mark with a pencil, remove the front cross rail and plane the bevel. Reassemble.

▲ **10** Make a form for bending the laminated back slats (see page 209). Stack together a ½-in. (12mm) thickness of veneer. Try these dry in the form and make any necessary adjustments. Apply glue and wrap the bundle of laminates in plastic so that they do not stick to the form. Clamp them in the form and allow to cure overnight. Repeat to make the remaining five slats.

▼ **11** Plane one of the laminate edges of each slat, using the form as a support. Alternatively, hold the laminate in the vise. Gauge the laminate strip to width, saw to the gauge line and plane the remaining edge. Mark the top, bottom and tenon shoulder line from the form.

◀ **12** Clamp the slats together to finish marking the tenons, then cut them. Note that the shoulder lines will be cut at the correct angle later.

▶ **13** Push the tenoned slats into the mortises on the top rail.

◀ **14** Mark a center line on the seat cross rail. Place the two center back slats in their fanned position on the seat cross rail. When you are happy with their position, mark it in pencil and hold the slats in place with C clamps. Scribe the tenon shoulder lines at the top of each slat. Remove them from the frame and pare the tenon shoulders to the scribed lines. The two slats can now be pushed home into the mortises.

▶ **15** The bottoms of the slats are narrowed where they are screwed to the seat cross rail; this allows the seat slats to fit between them. Mark the narrow part on the two center back slats. Mark the narrow point on the seat slat that will fit between them as well.

◀ **16** To get the curved edge on the narrow part, start with a drilled hole at the inner curve, then saw and finish the curve with a spokeshave.

▶ **17** Drill screw holes to attach the back slats to the seat cross rail. Alternatively, cut slots instead of holes, which will allow for any slight movement when sitting in the chair and will relieve the top tenons of any stress. Continue fitting the rest of the back slats in the same way. Notice that the mortise-and-tenons at the top of the back slats are not glued yet.

18 Starting with the center seat slat, narrow the slat where it will be screwed to the seat cross rail. Narrow the other slats and place in a fanned position. Mark the recesses for them on the front rail. Remove the rail from the frame and cut the recesses. This can be done either by hand with saw and chisels, or with a router.

19 Replace the front cross rail in the frame and fit the seat slats. Due to the curvature of the seat and front rails, the rear of the slats will not sit flat, so cut the angle to allow each slat to fit. Drill and screw in place.

20 Mark the length of each seat slat and trim if necessary to ensure that they fit snugly in the recesses on the front rail. Drill and screw in place.

21 Remove all screws, slats and so on, and sand all components (but do not remove your identification numbering). Assemble the main seat frame, apply glue to the joints on the three cross rails and clamp the frame. Check for squareness and wipe away excess glue. When the glue has cured, remove the clamps, mask the mortises on the top back rail and apply a finish. Mask the tenons on the top of the back slats, then sand and finish all slats. Install the back slats, applying glue and light clamping pressure to pull the mortise-and-tenons together. Screw the slats in place.

Dovetailed box

Precision marking and cutting are more important than ever when making small objects, because our eyes are drawn to look closely at joints, the way things are put together and the detailing. This box is made with through dovetailing, which acts as both a structural and visual feature. Only a small quantity of wood is needed for small items like this, so take the opportunity to choose an exciting and exotic wood. The prototype is made of yew because, although it is difficult to work, it has a lovely appearance.

Tool list

- Bar clamps
- Pencil; steel rule; marking knife; try square; marking gauge; mortise gauge
- Panel saw; dovetail saw; coping saw
- Jack or smoothing plane; block plane
- Power router, or rabbet plane or shoulder plane and hand router
- Small bevel-edged chisels
- Nail set
- Cabinet scraper; sandpaper and sanding block

Cutting list

No.	Sawn	Planed
2 long sides	7 1/2 x 3 1/2 x 3/4 in. (190 x 85 x 20mm)	7 x 3 x 1/2 in. (180 x 75 x 12mm)
2 short sides	5 1/2 x 3 1/2 x 3/4 in. (140 x 85 x 20mm)	5 x 3 x 1/2 in. (130 x 75 x 12mm)
1 top	7 x 5 x 3/4 in. (180 x 130 x 20mm)	6 1/2 x 4 1/2 x 5/8 in. (162 x 115 x 14mm)
1 bottom	7 x 5 x 1/2 in. (180 x 130 x 12mm)	6 1/2 x 4 1/2 x 3/8 in. (162 x 115 x 10mm)
Lining	Measure the insides of the finished box and cut 2 long sides and 2 short sides	

Plus: Panel or veneer pins; masking tape; glue; finishing materials; hinges (optional).

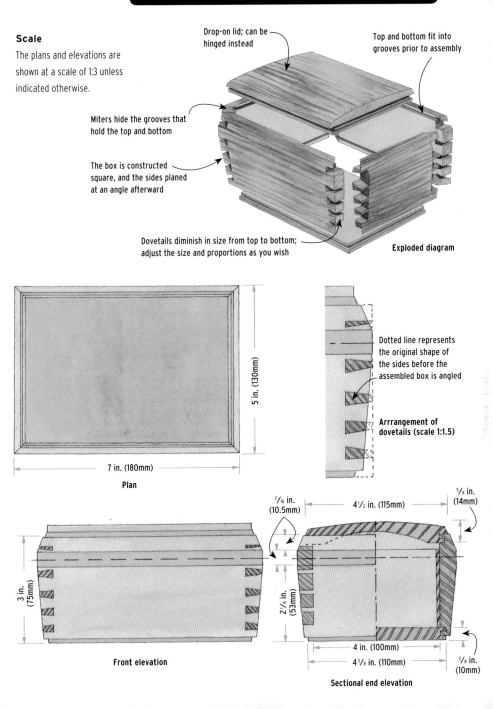

Scale

The plans and elevations are shown at a scale of 1:3 unless indicated otherwise.

Drop-on lid; can be hinged instead

Top and bottom fit into grooves prior to assembly

Miters hide the grooves that hold the top and bottom

The box is constructed square, and the sides planed at an angle afterward

Dovetails diminish in size from top to bottom; adjust the size and proportions as you wish

Exploded diagram

5 in. (130mm)

7 in. (180mm)

Plan

Dotted line represents the original shape of the sides before the assembled box is angled

Arrrangement of dovetails (scale 1:1.5)

3 in. (75mm)

Front elevation

7/16 in. (10.5mm)

4 1/2 in. (115mm)

5/8 in. (14mm)

2 1/8 in. (53mm)

4 in. (100mm)

4 3/8 in. (110mm)

3/8 in. (10mm)

Sectional end elevation

Corner to be mitered | Pins | Miter already cut

Groove | Groove

SEE ALSO
Holding and clamping, *pages 24–25*
Core tools and techniques, *pages 28–99*
Gluing and clamping, *pages 106–107*
Dovetail joints, *pages 132–137*
Finishes and fittings, *pages 172–185*

Making the box

▶ 1 Mark and cut all the components and plane them square; make the sides about 1/16 in. (1.5mm) over length. Cut the grooves along the top and bottom of each side piece. Mark and cut the pins on the two short sides of the box. Mark the miters at each corner, sawing about 1/16 in. (1.5mm) away from the marked line so that you can fit each corner snugly, paring where necessary. Leave one miter unsawn until you have marked the tails.

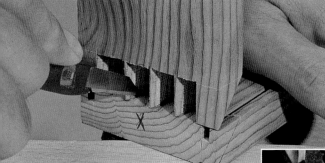

◀ 2 With the long sides on the bench, the inside face uppermost, position the cut pins and mark the tails from them. Use a clamp to make sure that the pieces do not move. Mark and cut the miters as before.

▶ 3 Cut the grooves in the top and bottom pieces that will allow them to fit into the grooves in the sides. The box top has a curved face; use a plane to shape it. Also plane a bevel on the sides of the top. If you wish, chisel out the inside of the lid; this is often done with small boxes to lessen the weight of the top.

▶ **4** Disassemble the four sides and check the fit of all parts. Sand and finish all inside surfaces, masking the joint surfaces of the dovetails. You can finish all grooves at this stage because the construction allows for a slight movement of the wood. Glue the joints and assemble the box, removing from the clamps when the glue has cured. Plane the outsides from their original rectangular shape; this gives the box some interest, especially in the apparent reduction in the size of the dovetails.

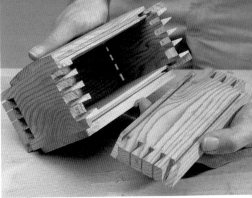

◀ **5** Gauge a line around the completed box where you want the lid to separate from the bottom.

▶ **6** Saw along the the gauged line, then plane the joining surfaces, so that the top fits the bottom exactly.

◀ **7** Carefully measure the inside of the box, including the lid cavity, and cut the linings to fit inside; they should fit as tight as possible without allowing them to bow. Miter them at the corners. Sand and finish the box. Here, the lining is stained a contrasting color. If you wish, install hinges.

Carved pumpkin box

Care and precision are needed to carve this box, but the result is very worthwhile. You can use any lightweight, easily carvable hardwood. For the prototype, three pieces of jelutong were carefully planed and glued together to form a suitably sized block to carve. You can adapt the design to any shape you like; you do not have to copy the pumpkin here exactly. The leaf, for example, has to be drawn onto the partially carved box freehand, which will help to make your box unique. The tooled finish on the inside of the box provides a satisfying contrast with the smoothly sanded outer skin.

SEE ALSO

Sawing, *pages 42–61*

Planing, *pages 62–71*

Sanding materials, *page 88*

Woodcarving, *pages 154–163*

Finishes, *pages 172–181*

Tool list

■ Pencil; steel rule; compass; marking knife

■ Handsaw

■ Jack or smoothing plane

■ Carving gouges and chisels; carving mallet

■ Cabinet scraper; sandpaper

Cutting list

1 block	8½ x 8½ x 6 in. (215 x 215 x 150mm)

Plus: Paper for sketches; cardboard for templates; finishing materials.

Making the box

▶ **1** Sketch the pumpkin shape and prepare full-size plan, side and sectional drawings. Mark a sawing line around the block 2½ in. (65mm) from the base, and saw through. Plane and scrape the sawn surfaces. Trace the outline of the plan view onto the surfaces; use one side of the tracing for the base section, and the other side for the lid section, so that they match when put together. Carefully hand-draw the outline shape ¼ in. (6mm) inside the traced shape to establish the width of the flange (base) and rabbet (lid).

◀ **2** Beginning with the base, set in the line of the flange. Start working parallel to it using a parting tool, then use appropriately shaped gouges to stab precisely up to the hand-drawn line to a depth of ¼ in. (6mm), taking care to make it flat and regular just inside the line, because this area will be the seating for the rabbet on the lid.

▶ **3** Make a cardboard profile template, cut at a right angle and to the correct depth. Run this along the flange to help you to check that it is accurate.

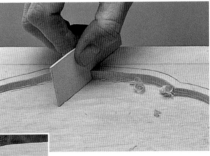

◀ **4** The lid must be a good fit. Using the template as a guide, set in the rabbet on the lid to a depth of ¼ in. (6mm). Test the fit of the lid at intervals.

◄ **5** You will now be able to put the halves together whenever necessary to assess progress or to carve across the join. Saw off the corners and rough out the cylindrical shape. Carve the two halves alternately, bringing them both to the same stage. Pin scrapwood blocks to the bench to help you hold the pieces as you carve.

► **6** Draw lines ¼ in. (6mm) within the flange to define the thickness of the walls. Using spoon gouges, begin to hollow out the base and the lid, while the top and bottom are still flat.

▼ **8** Draw the leaf on the top and set in the shape. Glue a small piece of wood to the top for the stem, with the grain running along its length. The free end will rest on the leaf, so orient it with care.

▲ **7** Rough out the shapes of the lid and base separately, using profile templates slightly larger than the final size to ensure that the overall shape progresses evenly. As you approach the final shape, make smaller gouge cuts to allow more subtle modeling of the forms.

9 Use spoon gouges to hollow out both halves. A finger and thumb, one inside and the other outside, provide an effective way of gauging thickness.

Flat portion on the base acts as a foot ring

Calyx

▶ **10** Sand the outside with coarse garnet paper to remove gouge marks and to continue rounding the forms. A foot ring must be left so that the box will sit flat, so draw two circles for its outer and inner limits. Set in the calyx at the center of the base. Continue sanding to remove the gouge marks and blend the forms.

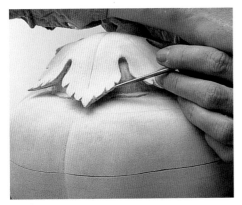

◀ **11** Carve in all the veins, indentations and other leaf details. Aim for a contrasting texture between the stem and the lively curving leaf. The modeling of the leaf surface is mainly achieved with sandpaper. Undercut the leaves to separate them visually from the fruit beneath.

▶ **12** Sand with coarse garnet paper, followed by fine, to complete the modeling and remove all the marks. Apply a finish. Here, the pumpkin box was sealed with three coats of special pale polish, followed by a light waxing.

Turned toadstools

Toadstools and mushrooms—or gnome homes and fairy houses as they are otherwise known—are a bit of woodturning fun, ideal for a beginner. There is no set pattern for them. They can be tall, short, fat or thin; try to make each one unique. They are mostly made from branch wood, to give them a natural edge. Polish with beeswax for a natural finish.

SEE ALSO
Sanding materials, *page 88*
Woodturning, *pages 164–171*
Finishes, *pages 172–181*

Tool list

- Woodturning lathe and chuck
- Spindle gouge; parting tool
- Coping saw
- Chisel or sharp knife
- Sandpaper

Cutting list

1 split-free, dry branch wood, such as yew	2½ in. (65mm) diameter x 6 in. (150mm) long
Plus: Friction polish	

Making a toadstool

1 Mount the blank between centers and use a parting tool to cut a spigot to suit your chuck.

◀ **2** Fit the chuck to the lathe, making sure that the spigot on the blank is firmly gripped in the chuck.

▶ **3** With the lathe turning at its top speed, cut the shape of the toadstool head with a spindle gouge. To create a gentle curve without any facets, start to cut and move the tool through to the center in one motion.

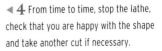

◀ **4** From time to time, stop the lathe, check that you are happy with the shape and take another cut if necessary.

◄ **5** Carefully sand and polish the head. Try not to round off the natural edge, because keeping it crisp makes the piece look a lot better. Make sure that you use some form of dust-extraction system while you sand.

▶ **6** Start cutting under the head, taking care that the wings of the tool do not catch as you proceed with the cut.

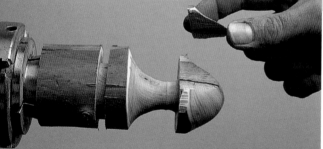

◄ **7** This is what can happen when you are not watching the wings of the tool carefully enough.

▶ **8** If you do have a disaster, part the damaged head off and start again with the spindle gouge. If you have trouble starting the cut because the tool skids away, use the parting tool to make an entry cut.

▶ **9** Shape the underside of the head, and cut a stem that tapers slightly from the base and has a small radius where it joins the head. This makes it easier to sand, and does not look as though the head were stuck on afterward.

◀ **10** Sand and polish the workpiece, making sure that you keep your fingers away from the natural edge.

▶ **11** Do not part the workpiece totally with the parting tool, but leave a small stub to saw through. You can then pare this away with a chisel or sharp knife.

Sleeping Dragon
Alun Heslop
This sinuous curving bench, designed to face
a garden pond, was constructed in oak and
stainless steel using carving, steam-bending
and composite jointing techniques.

7
Gallery

Inspirational examples of finished pieces
from professional woodworkers

Chairs and seating

▲ *Small Sofa*
Arthur and Rachel Cadman
The use of subtle curves in this small
sofa has produced an inviting and
cheerful piece of furniture. The frame
is made of cherry and is upholstered.

◀ *Wycliff Chair*
Paul Forrester

Based on a 1908 design by Leonard Wyburd, this chair is made from quartersawn oak and upholstered in antique leather. Its sharp angular lines work together in a way that makes the chair a lot stronger than it might look at first sight.

▶ *Lightweight Stacking Chairs*
Simon Smith

Smith's designs have a simplicity of form and well-defined lines that give his work a sharp and fresh presence. These stacking chairs have a lightweight steam-bent ash frame, and laminated and color-sprayed seat and back.

◀ *Ofido Stool and Magazine Rack*
Facundo Poj

The distinctive feature of Poj's work is the combination of bamboo plywood with CNC (computer numerical control) routing, enabling forms to be explored that would otherwise be impossible to achieve. The sections are glued and doweled together, and sprayed with a water-based finish—no nails, no screws.

▶ *Unstable Stool*
Angus Ross

The stool is Ross's first batch-produced product in his steam-bent range. The sculpted ash seat is supported by an asymmetric steam-bent rocker that places the user into the optimal seated pose when working at a desk.

▲ *Knot Chair*

John Makepeace

This chair is a work of art in its own right. The legs and arms are sculpted from laminated oak, while the cushions and knots are from burl elm, both bleached almost white. The ability to invoke such fluid textures into a piece of furniture is the work of a true master.

▼ *Arc Chair White*

Tom Raffield

Raffield and his collective, Sixixis, marry traditional techniques with contemporary design to produce beautiful furniture. In designing this chair, Raffield has pushed the boundaries of steam bending by introducing complex three-dimensional forms using unseasoned wood.

▲ *Razorfish*

Alun Heslop

This carved bench seat has been given an innovative twist by creating an overlapping saddle that invites people to sit on either side. Made in weathered oak, it is suitable for both exterior and interior locations.

◀ *Rolling Summerhouse*

Charlie Whinney

This extraordinary spherical structure is large enough to sit inside relaxing, but also light enough for an adult to roll around the garden.

Tables and desks

▲ ▶ *Mollusc*

John Makepeace

This desk is made with washed oak from trees planted in 1760 and felled in 1980. Opening the sliding writing surface reveals storage beneath. An internal curved oak beam connects the three legs.

▲ *Embrace*
David Tragen

This table is made from cherry, the individual pieces being routed using a template. With its glass top, the interlocking design creates fascinating shadows when lit from above.

▼ *Sagrada Table*
Derek Elliott

The arched legs of this table were inspired by the Sagrada Família cathedral in Barcelona, the unfinished masterpiece of Spanish architect Antoni Gaudí. The arched legs are brick-constructed from solid oak; the tabletop is veneered.

▲ *Console Table*
Silverlining
This desk is made in English elm and
shagreen leather. It is the exquisite use of
chip carving on the external surfaces that
makes the piece so distinctive.

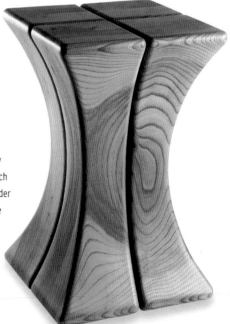

▶ *Check*
Peter Cummings
This simple but elegant form was achieved by
laminating four identical sections of elm, which
were then shaped using jigs on a spindle molder
equipped with a ring fence. The sections were
butt-jointed together using dowels.

▲ ▼ *Games Table*

Rupert McBain

This scrabble table was designed for a superyacht, so it needed to be stable in a marine environment. The central games board rotates within a raised silver-plated rim, and locks in the quarter positions. Details such as handles were made in calf leather and cast nickel silver plate.

Cabinets, shelving and storage

▶ *Watch Winder*
Silverlining
This truly luxurious watch
winder is made from ebony,
rosewood, satinwood, walnut
and gold. The contemporary
use of marquetry over three-
dimensional shapes adds to
the drama of the piece.

▼ *Wobbly Sideboard in Polstead Oak*
Dylan Pym
Traditional techniques, such as handcut pegs and steam
bending, were used to make this sideboard from oak and
chestnut. The doors open on swivel-action pins.

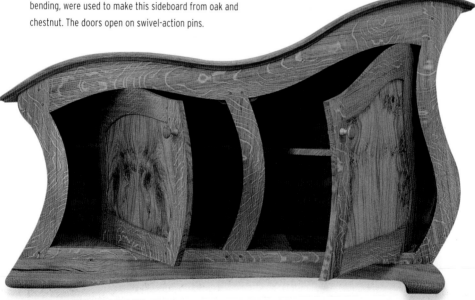

▼ ► *Flow*

John Makepeace

This boldly detailed cabinet is constructed from rippled ash, with the grain matching at each corner. The drawer linings are of holly, cedar and oak. With exceptional skill, Makepeace has reflected the patterns you would find on a beach in this piece of furniture.

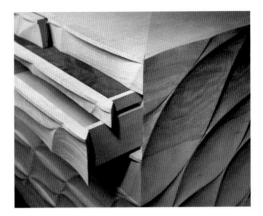

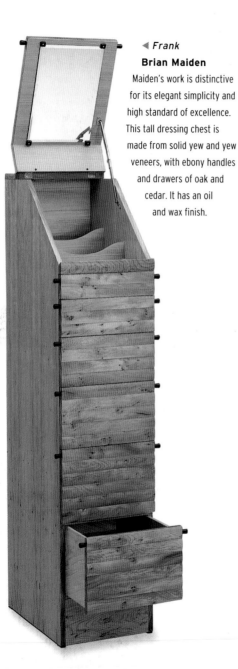

◀ *Frank*
Brian Maiden

Maiden's work is distinctive for its elegant simplicity and high standard of excellence. This tall dressing chest is made from solid yew and yew veneers, with ebony handles and drawers of oak and cedar. It has an oil and wax finish.

▲ *Soldier's Cabinet*
Derek Elliott

This cabinet gets its name from the inlay on the doors, which was inspired by the kind of decoration that might have been found on a cavalry tunic. The architectural shape owes a great deal to Japanese joinery. The cabinet is made from walnut.

▼ ▶ *Wye Bridge*

Tim Hawkins

This wine cabinet was inspired by a bridge in
Hawkins' native city. Made of cherry and walnut,
their rich colors convey a sense of the warm touch
of local sandstone. The uprights hold shelves for
storing bottles, while the two doors between the
uprights provide storage space for glasses.

▶ *Swirl*

Arthur and Rachel Cadman

The elegant swirl detail on this cabinet was created by steam bending sweet chestnut to form a curved rail. Other sections were made by veneering and laminating.

▼ *Crossing Over*

Anthony Scheffler

Scheffler combines exotic woods with a range of metals to produce distinctive pieces that explore simple forms with intersecting lines and angles. This magazine holder is made from congona, bloodwood and anodized aluminum.

▲ *Fireland Flow*

David Tragen

Fireland Flow was made to the dimensions of a Buddhist altar using lenga and
padauk veneers, and was designed as a showpiece for exhibitions. The cabinet
shows considerable subtlety in its details, in particular the handle grips.

▲ *Spacejunk Eclipse*
Michael Hindmarsh

This shelving unit combines bold design and simplicity
of form with humor—the use of two colors to suggest
an eclipse is a witty detail. Techniques used include
CNC (computer numerical control) routing of the
components, which were then mitered and
half-slotted together.

◀ *Display Cabinet*
Sean Feeney

The solid sections of this glazed
sycamore cabinet are curved to the
same radius and bonded together with
biscuit joints. The unit incorporates
concealed low-voltage lighting.

Paul Forrester

This bookcase has hammered copper hinges on the lower cupboard, and a traditional leaded light panel on the upper one. Made from solid French quartersawn oak that is known to be over 400 years old, the design is loosely based on an original by Leonard Wyburd and sold through Liberty's of London.

Decorative woodwork

◀ *Buckeye Burl Hollow Form*
Ron Overholtz

This is an ambitious piece of woodturning in a difficult and unforgiving wood. From this piece of burl, Overhlotz has produced an ultra-thin, but strong and elegant form.

▼ *Cutlery Stand*
Marcus Mindelsohn

Inspired by old knife and hat boxes, the main body of the stand was laminated from handcut veneers of brown and tiger oak, and the outer case was laminated with rippled sycamore veneer and blue-stained maple.

▲ *Giant Curly Lampshade*
Charlie Whinney
This striking centerpiece is a fine example of
what can be achieved with steam bending.

◀ ▶ *Ascension*
Don Freas
Freas successfully combines
storytelling, poetry and sculpture
in his woodwork. The piece is
made from Douglas fir, walnut,
mahogany, maple and corkscrew
willow. The open column is a
jointed construction, while the
hanging figure is hand-carved.

Glossary

Across the grain At 90 degrees to the grain direction of the wood. On most boards, this would be across the width of the piece.

Against the grain Working in a direction that forces the wood to split along the direction of the grain downward into the wood.

Air-dried Wood dried without the application of artificial heat.

Bevel A flat, angled surface, planed or carved on the edge of a board. A bevel of 45 degrees is called a miter.

Bird's eye Small circular patterns in the wood surface that resemble a bird's eyes and that are caused by conical depressions; found in maple and other woods.

Blank A piece of wood prepared for turning on a lathe.

Burl A highly figured section of wood or veneer, with tight swirling grain, cut from an abnormal growth that develops on the trunks of some trees.

Burr A thin ridge of metal left on a blade's cutting edge after grinding or honing. Some tools, such as a cabinet scraper, require a burr to function; others, such as a chisel, do not.

Checks Tiny splits along the length of the board, often caused by improper drying procedures.

Coarse grain Wood with wide, visible growth rings.

Countersinking Enlarging the upper part of a bored hole so that a screw head can be set beneath the surface of the wood.

Crosscutting Sawing a board across its width or grain.

Cross-grain construction Any construction where a long-grain section of wood is fastened across the grain of another piece, thereby restricting wood movement.

Dado A channel cut across the grain. A wide dado is sometimes called a trench; a deep dado is sometimes called a notch.

Earlywood The lighter section of a growth ring, formed at the beginning of the growing season.

End grain Grain section at the end of a board.

Face side/edge The most attractive side or edge of a board, generally positioned where it will be most visible in a piece of furniture.

Fence Adjustable guide against which the wood is held to ensure that it remains a set distance from the cutting edge of a machine.

Figure The decorative pattern on a wood surface that is caused by grain, color variations, branch growth, injury, interlocked fibers, growth stresses or other factors.

Fine grain Wood with narrow, fairly inconspicuous growth rings.

Form A mold used for bending and shaping laminates.

Grain The pattern visible on the wood surface that is due to the growth rings and the angle at which the board was sliced from the tree.

Green wood Freshly cut wood that has not been dried.

Groove A channel cut along the grain of the wood.

Growth rings Concentric rings formed under the bark of trees growing in temperate zones. Tropical trees grow constantly, so growth rings are not generally visible.

Hardwood Wood from a tree with broad leaves (deciduous) that are usually shed in the fall.

Heartwood The darker section of wood extending from the center of the tree (the pith) to the sapwood.

Jig A device, either proprietary or workshop-made, that is used to hold or guide the wood being worked or the tool being used. Jigs help you to carry out a task with greater accuracy, and to repeat that task to make identical pieces.

Kerf Width of groove left by a saw blade.

Kickback When a workpiece is thrown back toward the operator when using a machine tool, or a handheld power tool jumps backward.

Kiln-dried Wood dried with artificial heat in a large oven-like structure called a kiln.

Knot Section of branch embedded in a board. Dark, loose knots are generally referred to as dead knots.

Laminate Two or more layers (laminations) of wood glued together; can be bent using a form.

Latewood The darker section of a growth ring, formed at the end of the growing season.

Medullary rays Horizontal rays radiating from the center of the tree, perpendicular to the growth rings.

Miter An angle of 45 degrees.

Moisture content The amount of moisture that is present in wood, expressed as a percentage. Moisture levels change constantly in response to changes in the relative humidity of the environment.

Mortise A hole, usually rectangular, cut into a piece of wood to accept a tenon. A through mortise extends right through the wood; a stopped or blind mortise does not.

Rabbet A recess or step cut along the edge of a board.

Rail The horizontal component of a frame.

Ripping Sawing down the length of a board, with the grain.

Sapwood Growing wood section near the outside of the tree. This is usually a lighter color than the heartwood.

Seasoning The process of drying wood to reduce its moisture content. Air-drying and kiln-drying methods are commonly used.

Shakes Splits between adjacent layers of wood fibers, usually caused by growth stresses or improper drying. Similar to checks, but usually wider and longer.

Softwood Wood from needle-leafed trees, usually evergreens (conifers), that bear their seeds in cones.

Spline A thin piece of wood glued into mating grooves of components to be joined together.

Stile The vertical component of a frame.

Stop A device used to stop the wood or tool from moving farther than the required position.

Tearout Torn wood fibers caused by a blade as it exits a cut.

Tenon A projection, usually rectangular, cut at the end of a rail for insertion into a mortise.

Tongue A projection of wood cut along the edge of a board that interlocks with a matching groove on the adjoining edge of another board.

Waney edge Natural unsawn edge of a board.

Warping Distortion of wood caused by improper seasoning or cutting, or growth factors. The most common forms are bowing, producing a bend along the length of the piece; cupping, creating a hollow across the width; and twisting, where the corners are not in the same plane.

Index

Credits

We would like to thank the following people and companies for kindly supplying images for inclusion in this book:

Arthur and Rachel Cadman *www.cadmanfurniture.com*
Peter Cummings *www.petercummings.co.uk*
Derek Elliott *www.outofthewood.co.uk*
Sean Feeney *www.seanfeeneyfurniture.co.uk (Photo: Chris Challis)*
Don Freas *www.donfreas.com*
Tim Hawkins *www.finefurniture.co.uk*
Alun Heslop *www.chaircreative.com*
Michael Hindmarsh *www.mikehindmarsh.co.nz*
Rupert McBain *www.rupertmcbainfurniture.co.uk*
Brian Maiden *www.brianmaiden.com*
John Makepeace *www.johnmakepeacefurniture.com*
Marcus Mindelsohn *www.mgmfinefurniture.co.uk*
Ron Overholtz *www.overholtzwoodturnings.com*
Facundo Poj *www.facundopoj.com*
Dylan Pym *www.dylanpym.co.uk*
Tom Raffield *www.tomraffield.com*
Angus Ross *www.angusross.co.uk*
Anthony Scheffler *www.anthonyscheffler.com*
Silverlining *www.silverliningfurniture.co.uk (Photo: Mark Reeves Photography)*
Simon Smith *www.simonsmithfurniture.com*
David Tragen *www.tragendesign.com*
Charlie Whinney *www.charliewhinney.com*

Paul Forrester would like to thank Marcus Mindelsohn for his help with advice and practical applications.